EARLY HEDGESVILLE CHRONICLES

YEARS 1720 – 1947

WILLIAM D. MOORE

NORTH MOUNTAIN PRESS

MARTINSBURG, WV

This book is dedicated to

My Wife, Mary Kate

&

My Daughter, Laura

CONTENTS

Hedgesville – at the gap of the mountain

THE SPRING & THE MOUNTAIN GAP

The Town of Hedgesville is located in the Gap of the North Mountain range and really is the beginning of that range that extends about 24 miles south. The town is located in Berkeley County, West Virginia.

There are several gaps in the mountain and later settlers gave them names but the early Indians and wild game knew the water from the spring long before that time. It was the first gap in the mountain from the Valley floor that had a gentler slope and a path through the hills.

The area was an unbroken wilderness and that was later broken for the paths of the buffalo and later the trails of the many tribes of Indians who came to the area to hunt.

"The trails were later given names and branches of them existed: the Seneca, Pocahontas and the Warrior Path. The latter became a trader's and explorer's route in ascending the Shenandoah Valley. "

Although there is no evidence to support it, there is cause to speculate that perhaps the spring area was once an" Indian village" as they usually located a spot upon an elevated area near a spring."

There was an Indian tribe that did exist in the area and that was the Tuscarora tribe. In 1713 they became one of the confederated tribes which became known as the Six Nations.

You can find their name still listed as the Tuscarora Presbyterian Church and for the name of the creek that still flows. They were a large tribe but suddenly left the area in the 1750's at the instigation of the French and went westward toward the Alleghenies.

The area was a favored hunting ground of the Indian. Wild game such as buffalo, deer, elk, bear, fox and others were found in abundance. Wild birds were plentiful, as duck, geese, quail, and grouse while the streams teemed with freshwater fish.

Other Indian tribes came into the area to hunt. It was during this time that they were not allowed to war with each other and so a general peace ensued. The valley floor would be thick with vegetation and they would burn off vast stretches of it so they could navigate around. The different tribes would gather around common springs and during this time there was to be no conflict or war.

"The main groups to frequent West Virginia were the Shawnee from southern Ohio, the Mingos from Pennsylvania, the Delaware from eastern Pennsylvania, the Seneca - part of the Iroquois... and others wandered the area.

The never failing spring from which Hedgesville garnered its reason for being is one of several large springs that are from the same aquifer. Jones Spring, Tomahawk Spring, and the Town Spring , Ben Speck Spring, Harlan Springs and Bedington Spring .... all are formed from a common source.

"There are four historical gaps by which the North Mountain is crossed in Berkeley County. From North to South, they are: Skinners Gap (Hedgesville), Parks Gap to Tomahawk, Boyd's Gap, and Mills Gap (to Gerrardstown) "

Almost everyone entering the village sees the metal highway sign placed there by the state of West Virginia to give historical significance to the site.
It says: "HEDGESVILLE - Site of stockade

fort built during the early Indian wars. Mt Zion Episcopal Church was built soon after. A mile west is the tavern built 1740-1750 by Robert Snodgrass on land patented in 1732 by William Snodgrass pioneer settler. "

It brings to mind that the area was gripped in the savage fighting of the French & Indian War as the French inflamed the Indians to eradicate settlers from their "hunting grounds"

Several pioneer stockade forts were established where families could run to for safety and security when the Indians set out with raiding groups. "About the year 1756 there were many raids by the Indians who destroyed everything they could by murdering the inhabitants and burning their property. "

These stockade forts were established at Ft. Evans two miles south of Martinsburg; Fort Neally near the mouth of the Opequon River; one partially completed fort in Martinsburg; and Fort Hedges on the west side of Back Creek.

This brings us to the supposition that

perhaps the stockade fort was near Johnson-town .... Or if the cardinal directions were incorrect, the stockade fort could have been located at the Hedges farm outside of the village in the opposite direction. In any case, no one has definitely located where the stockade fort was, but its history has been named, identified, and forged in metal for all to recall.

One incident did occur at Snodgrass Tavern that underlines the area's dangerous, perilous time. It happened during the infancy of Elizabeth Snodgrass, eldest daughter of Robert & Susannah Rawlings Snodgrass. One day when the mother was alone with her baby, she saw the Indians approaching the house. She took the baby into a pit under the floor boards with a hope of saving their lives, but with the intention of smothering the baby should it, by crying, disclose their hiding place to the Indians.

While the marauding Indians drank and fought above her head, blood trickled down through the floor boards on her body. She feared her husband had returned and had been murdered by the Indians.

After a time when all had become quiet, she

came from her hiding place and found the dead body to be that of an Indian and not her husband. Her husband returned late that evening and together they buried the Indian.

The original Snodgrass Tavern
Hedgesville, WV

SETTLEMENT OF THE TOWN

Hedgesville became civilized as time went by as did the rest of the mix of peoples who flooded into the area by migration. It began in the 1720's and continued beyond the 1830's.

Listen to the over-embellished, contrived spelling, and inventive words that has been taken from the Martinsburg Gazette, Martinsburg February 2, 1832 to describe Hedgesville:

"It may not be amiss to state for the information of the public, that the site for a village to be called by the above name, has lately been laid off on Mr. Josiah Hedges land upon the North mountain, contiguous to Mt. Zion church (lately Hedges Chapel) and added intersection of Sir John's with the Warm Springs Road. For salubrity of atmosphere pure, refreshing, and never failing fountain water, this site for a village has not a rival for many miles around; and these are very desirable objects to every person. Here a sojourn from harvest till the appearance of frosted October, would, in all probability, avert disease and prolong life and here might be the valetudinarians of the

Valley resort during the summer and autumn months, drink of the life-giving elements, and inhale the PURE and invigorating mountain air with the most happy result.

The fact is that among the earliest citizens of the immediate vicinity, more instances of advanced age and extreme longevity can be enumerated, than perhaps any other part of Berkeley can boast of, all things considered and who would not make an effort to guard against the periodical attacks of the bilious fever, and the horrible train of consequences that have arrested almost a countless number of all ages, and hurried them to a premature grave since 1808?

In another point of view, this place is worthy of notice. Owing to the want of a convenient seminary of learning, conducted and superintended by distinguished masters in scientific attainments, have scores of native students of the adjacent country grown to manhood and are advancing to old age, without having their minds cultivated, enlightened and embellished by the beauties of classic lore; nor by the preparatory acquisition of mathematical truth. An establishment of this sort, at this spot, is much wanted, and would, undoubtedly meet with adequate support.

The view westward of the village, although some sterile, presents a surface pleasingly diversified, with hill and dale covered with dense, and salutiferous (healthy) growth of Evergreen. The county in that direction, for many miles, offers the most fascinating inducements to gentlemen fond of the pleasures of the chase. To the eastward as far as the blue Mountains the eyes feast in wandering over the beautiful, fertile and extended playing on both sides of the Potomac, with the undulating variegated and charming surface ornamented with numerous and well cultivated farms and farmhouses.

This village we are building has already commenced and is progressing is 7 miles from Martinsburg, 18 from Bath, and 12 from Williamsport."

THE *TOWN* OF HEDGESVILLE ESTABLISHED

The village of Hedgesville was laid out as town in the 1830's, established by the General Assembly of Virginia in 1836, and incorporated by the General Assembly in 1854.

In 1832, Josiah Hedges decided he would lay off some of his land into lots and establish the village which would be called Hedgesville. On November 3, 1832 he sold the first lots, which were lots eight and nine to his brother Hezekiah Hedges for $60; these lots contained 1/4 acre each and were located on Main Street --- the warm Springs Road --- and what was then called Cross Street.

Deed book 41 page 294 Josiah Hedges and wife Catherine, to Thomas J Harley for $30 on the 9 September 1835 a lot of land in Hedgesville on the road from Martinsburg to Bath lot 10 fronting on Main Street and cross street along Lot 11.

Deed book 41 page 112 3 November 1832 to Josiah Hedges and Kathryn to Thomas Davis for $30 Lot 11 in Hedgesville in the gap of the North Mountain on the Warm Springs Road on Main Street.

Deed book 4 page 237, 9 September 1835 - Josiah Hedges senior and Kathryn to Philip Clawingen for $40 two certain lots in the town of Hedgesville, lot five and six fronting on Main Street the original line of the Hedges patent line along Lot 6.

Deed book 41, September 9, 1835 Josiah Hedges senior and Kathryn to James Cox for $20, lot number for a long Philip C Cloninger and Lot 5 along the line of Mary Claycom and Josiah Hedges to the west side of cross street to Main Street.

Deed book 43 page 404 19 September 1839 Josiah Hedges and Kathryn and Samuel Robinson for $30 a long alley with Cross Street to Valentine Runk.

Deed book 43 page 383 11 May 1839 Josiah Hedges and Kathryn his wife to Samuel Light a lot in Hedgesville beginning at the original division line between Josiah Hedges and John Westenhaver to Samuel Light.

Deed book 44 page 51 - 11 May 1839 Josiah Hedges and wife to Catherine Samuel Light or $13, lot in Hedgesville beginning at a stake in the original dividing line between Josiah Hedges and John Westenhaver and corner to Philip Clowinger lot to George Swisher corner nine.

Deed book 44 page 53 - 11 May 1839 Josiah Hedges and wife Philip C Clowinger along with John Westenhaver and Samuel Robinson lot number seven to Samuel Lights corner.

Deed book 45 page 153 - 14 April 1841 Josiah Hedges and wife Catherine to Jacob Siebert for $30 lot Friday church street along Samuel Robinson to the northwest, 1/4 acre.

Due to some unpleasant happenings, Conrad Claycomb and his wife, Mary, had a legal separation on 23 June 1812; their separation is recorded on deed book 25, page 295. Mary was to receive $200 annually to be held in trust for her use by George Craiglow. She also was to receive it anytime she asked, a chaff bed, with a feather bed cover to go over it. She was to live with whoever she pleased as a free, unmarried woman. She was not to go to Conrad's house unless he asked for her. In 1813 Mary Claycomb purchased for $396, 72 acres from John Westenhaver and his wife Catherine.

The lines of the land ran alongside Hedges Chapel, George Creighlow two runners run to the intersection of Runner road with the Warm Springs Roads to Hedges, deed book 25, page 24. Conrad Claycomb furnished supplies during the revolution. He owned several hundred acres near the present Cumbo section of Berkeley County.

Mary Claycomb had decided in 1836 to divide the part of her land which joined Josiah Hedges into lots. She gave most of her lots to her children. This part of the village became known as Mary Claycomb's Improvement to Hedgesville. Lot 1, she gave to her son Frederick, who married Catherine Tabor, daughter of Adam Tabor, beginning at the East line of Mary streets toward the church to the lots of Hedgesville. Lot 2 she gave to her daughter Barbara who had married Jacob Myers. Lot 3 - Mary reserved for her own use. Lot 4 she gave to her daughter Kathryn who had married Job Robbins. Lot 5 she gave to her daughter Elizabeth who had married John Green. Lot # ? began at the corner of Mary Street on 16 January 1836. On 17 June 1837, Mary Claycomb sold for $17 to Benjamin Darby, John M Wolfe, John S Light, Philip C Clovinger and Henry Myers, trustees one half

Lot 7 which contained one rod and 9 1/2 links .... warehouse or place of worship was to be erected for the use of the members of the Methodist Episcopal Church in the United States of America.

[The present brick building was erected soon after and is one of the oldest Methodist buildings standing in Berkeley County; it became known as the Old Brick Church. After services were discontinued, it was purchased by Mr. A. D. Naylor and given to the town of Hedgesville]

Lot 6 she sold to Conrad Hedges deed book 43, page 427 12 January 1839 Mary Claycomb sold to her daughter Mary Myers [who had married John Myers] Lot 13 containing 9 acres along Lot 12 on the side of Hedgesville Road leading to the forks of Hedgesville and Sir John's Road. On January 12, 1838 Mary Claycomb gave her stone house home with 12 acres to her son-in-law John Myers, the tract of land join with the lands of Josiah Hedges, George Craiglow and the lot the Mount Zion Church, deed book 43 page 429. On 20 October 1851 widow Anna Mary Claycomb Myers and her only child Effa Evalina Myers, gave her house and all their land and slave, including what Anna Mary had received from her father, Conrad Claycomb, to the son of Kathryn Claycomb Robbins, deed book 54 page 120.

[The present Mary Street was named after this Mary Claycomb who was a very progressive woman in her day. Not only weathering a divorce, she became a land entrepreneur and sold off her lots contiguous to other people so that a simple village was laid out. Her Stone house still stands in 2015 immediately across from the Hedgesville elementary school]

Mary Claycomb's land reserved lot three was divided in half; in part sold to Mary Folch and Mary a. Ropp and the other half to John Siler on April 20, 1853. John Siler's children sold to James W. Welsh a certain house and a half lot along lot four. On 13 October 1860 James M & Elizabeth ? sold to Asa Jenkins for $1500 on October 1869. Jenkins executor, or another Jenkins, sold the lot to William M. Lemen. It was then sold to James A. Robinson 20 December 1890. On 22 November 1897 it was sold to Charles M. Brown. Here the Browns operated the post office and later a funeral business. The property was sold to James Brown's children

24 November 1939; then it was sold to Brady E Shriver who sold it to Mrs. Ethel Runkles May, 1960 .

John Green's daughter, Mary Ann, married Jacob R. Miller February 1832. Jacob died and Marianne married a Mr. Cornelius - Barry Cornelius died in 1883 leaving the following children; Levi S. Miller, Mahala E. Miller, William M Miller, John Harley Miller and George Cornelius. Mary Cornelius sold the old Tavern at the corner of Main and Mary Street to John H. Miller who had returned the Tavern into a store. Mr. George Craglow ran the store for several years. In 1911 a special commissioner appointed by the court sold the store to J H Shipper - deed book 126, page 5 and 11 May 1911. J H shipper and wife Jeannie sold the old Tavern to Mr. James Poisal of the appraisal 7 December 1939 Deed book 167, page 171 [most of the building is log including part of the second story and may be the original old Tavern]

On 1 December 1857, Conrad K. Robbins and wife sold part of their land to Sally B. ? who sold in January 1866 to John M Speck. He sold it for $400 to Thomas L. Harley, Jacob Raab, and Thomas L Harper who constituted the Board of School Commissioners for the Hedgesville Township, one acre. This land lay on the borderline of Kreglow's land. A schoolhouse was erected soon after and was the Hedgesville School for many years

When the village of Hedgesville was incorporated in 1854, part of John Westenhaver's land was included. On 10 April 1847, John Westenhaver and wife, Mary, sold for $17 to Philip P Cloninger, Garrett Wynkoop, James Ijams, James Cox, and Valentine Runk, trustees of the schoolhouse of the town of Hedgesville, a lot of ground adjoining the town on the south side deed book 50 page 298; apparently the school was already there for Mr. Thomas Newton Lemon recorded in his daybook 21 December 1841: " load of wood to Mr. Canby, teacher of Hedgesville. " Mr. Westenhaver sold off several lots and after he died Henry J Seibert executor of his will, continued to sell lots. Shortly before his death Mr. Westenhaver did start to build a stone house near the town spring. John Westenhaver died February 1852. The house was purchased by Mr. William McKee 26 February 1853. Mr. McKee finished the lovely stone house and sold it for $1000 for a certain stone house and lot number 16 in the town of Hedgesville to Jacob Ferrel, who sold the house 13 July 1859 to William Rickard who gave it to Mr. James S Pitzer.

The Hedgesville area and town due to its location on the old wagon road from Alexandria to the Warm Springs and the lovely scenic views had been known since very early time for its taverns and hotels.

When Hezekiah Hedges married November 20, 1824 Elizabeth Snodgrass, he acquired the old Snodgrass Tavern and also built a mansion house with the store on lots eight and nine of Hedgesville. The Summit Hotel located at the south side of Main Street on the corner was built in the 1830s. John Siler acquired several lots in Hedgesville and much land on the west side of back Creek. In the division of John Siler's land the Summit Hotel was assigned to John T Siler and William L Tabor and Margaret Siler his wife. In 1868 they sold the hotel and store to Dr. James L Johnson, trustee of Van Johnson, His wife and Dr. Johnson used the old hotel as his home and for a short while it was a girls school with the name Summit Hall.

On the east side of the Episcopal Church stood another house that was built in the early 1840s. In 1841, Jacob Hull purchased two lots on Main Street adjoining the Episcopal Church from Josiah Hedges and his wife Catherine. Mr. Hull's wife was Elizabeth Siebert, daughter of Michael Siebert. In 1879, Jacob Hull gave the house to his three daughters: Elizabeth, Evalina, and Catherine Hull. Evalina married an Indian ,"George" Bushotter and continued living in the house. In 1923 Evalina Bushotter sold the property to Charles and Lucy Eversole who sold in 1971 to William and Mary Kate Moore. During the peak years of Mount Clifton Hotel, Evalina Bushotter took in boarders and overflow from the hotel and it was called the Summit House.

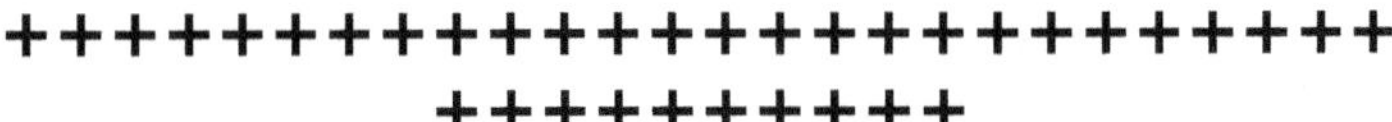

On the **30th of December 1835**, a **petition** was sent to the General Assembly asking that the **Village of Hedgesville** be established as a town. It reads:

To the Honorable General Assembly of Virginia - - -

Whereas we the undersigned citizens of Hedgesville being desirous to have a law establishing a town by the foregoing name, on the lands of Josiah Hedges senior and Mrs. Mary Claycomb, in the County of Berkeley on the public road leading from Martinsburg in said county, to the Berkeley Springs in the County of Morgan, 15 acres of land being surveyed and laid off for that purpose into lots with convenient streets and alleys and 15 good buildings in the place as also to appoint a suitable number of trustees for the government of said town, we therefore pray your honorable body favor us with a hearing nothing doubting that that you will favorably accept our petition, etc, and we will ever pray etc.

Josiah Hedges Senr
her Mary X Claycomb Mark

John Green
James Cox
Alfred Lucas
Robert Hedges
Samuel Robinson
Wesley Chambers
George W Robbins
Jacob M Seibert
James Shields
Alexander Robinson
Israel Tinning
James Curtis
Israel Norington
Benjamin C. Speck
Samuel Miller
Samuel Hedges the fourth
Edward winning
Hezekiah Hedges
John H. Spohn
Joseph Hedges
Harvey A. Hedges
Samuel H Shipley
Thomas J Harley
Janifer Chew Campbell
Peter Reiner
Michael Siebert
John Bear
William Hite
John Stevens
Jacob S.Underke

Daniel Weller
Henry Myers
George Kreglow
James Robinson
Thomas Harper
Philip C. Clowinger

A By Law imposing taxes in the Town of Hedgesville for the year 1836.

1. Be it ordained and declared by the Trustees of the Town of Hedgesville, that that the taxes to be assessed by the Trustee's ... on all the inhabitants and all property within the Bounds of said town, for the purpose authorized by law for the year 1836, shall be as follows to wit: two per cent of Houses and lots on every hundred dollars of the yearly rent thereof. Agreeably to the Books of the Commission of the revenue for Berkeley County for the year 1836 and in the same proportion for a quarter, or less sum, on all tithable persons fifty cents to be ascertained by the Books aforesaid.

2. Be it further enacted and declared by said trustees that the taxes hereby assessed and foresaid shall be collected by the collector

appointed by this Board and paid on or before the Ist. Day of December in each year into the hands of the Treasurer to be subject to the order of the President of the Board for the purpose of defraying the expenses of the Town of Hedgesville.

James Cox is appointed by this Board, Collector, for the town of Hedgesville for one year, who is required to give
Bond and security, to double the probable amount to be collected ....

Dr. Thomas J. Hartley is appointed by this Board, Treasurer for the Town of Hedgesville, who is also required to give Bond & Security, the same amount as the collector.

With the coming of the railroad and the establishment of a depot at North Mountain, the question of moving the Hedgesville Post Office to North Mountain arose. The inhabitants resented this suggestion and the Northern Republic of August 16, 1843 announced that a "public meeting would be held at Hedgesville against the removal of the Post Office from Hedgesville to the Iron Horse on the Railroad, to be held at Captain Hedges Hotel in Hedgesville."

After three years of discussion, the Virginia Free Press announced that the Post Office at the Depot on the Baltimore & Ohio Railroad, known as the Hedgesville Post Office, has been changed in name to that of the North Mountain Post Office and a new office has been opened in the Town of Hedgesville, bearing its name. Mr. P. H. Cookus is Post Master at the North Mountain Post Office and Mr. Mussetter at Hedgesville

THE ACT OF INCORPORATION

The following act incorporating the Town of Hedgesville was passed on March 1, 1854 in Virginia:

1. Be it enacted by the General Assembly of Virginia, that the corporate limits of the Town of Hedgesville, in the county of Berkeley, shall be laid and hereby established as follows: Beginning at a take on the west side of Martinsburg & Bath Road, near the corner of James R. Robinson's barnyard lot; thence north, twenty-nine and three fourths east, twenty eight and three tenths poles to a locust tree, near the north corner of the graveyard; thence north nine degrees, east twelve and one-tenth poles to a stake; thence north fifty two degrees, west seventy one and five tenths poles, to a black oak corner of John Bears and Mrs. Gilpin's; thence south forty degrees, west thirty one and four tenths poles, to the middle of the Potomac and Hedgesville Turnpike Road; thence along a line of same forty six and half degrees, west eleven and two tenths poles to a stake corner to same; thence with another their lines south thirty-five

degrees, east twenty eight poles, to a stake corner to Zorn, _insel, McKees, and Nicodemus; thence with McKees & Nicodemus line south fifty four degrees, west twenty six degrees and eight tenth poles, to a stake corner to same, and is in a line of Mose Nadenbousch; thence with said line south fifty and a half degrees, west twenty eight poles to a stake in said Nadenbousch's fields; thence, south thirty-nine and three fourth degrees, east fifty four pokes. To a stake near the north west base of the North Mountain; thence north forty-seven and three fourth degrees, east forty three square poles; and the same shall be and is hereby made a town corporation by the name of the "The Town of Hedgesville" and that that name shall have and exercise power conferred upon towns by the fifty-fourth chapter of the Code of Virginia. And be subject to all provision of said Chapter of the Code.

2. The officers of said town shall consist of seven trustees, who shall compose the Council, four of whom can act, and a sergeant; who shall hold their offices for one year and until their successors are appointed.

3. Jacob S. Stayer, Henry Hull, and George W. Snyder or any two of them, are hereby authorized to hold an election of the first Monday in May next, for the officers aforesaid, said election shall be conducted agreeably to the aforesaid chapter of the Code of Virginia.

4. Elections of officers aforesaid shall be held annually at the first Monday in the month of May.

5. This act shall be in force from its passage

In 1858 - the section of the act was amended to read as follows:

2. The officers of said Town (Hedgesville) shall consist of a Mayor and seven trustees, who shall compose the Council, four of whom can act, and a sergeant, who shall hold their offices for one year, and until their successors shall be elected.

A local Martinsburg newspaper of the time records that Hedgesville was a very industrious town in 1858. It had two tanneries, a saddle shop, a wagon maker, a merchant tailor, two hotels, two public and many private schools.

CHURCHES IN THE TOWN

Mt. Zion Episcopal Church - originally known as "Hedges Chapel" the congregation was founded in the 1740's. The log structure, which was beyond the present brick building on the rise of the hill, was visited by George Washington while on a surveying expedition for Lord Fairfax in 1750. The visit is mentioned in his diary.

A survey of the adjoining tract of land on 14 September 1752 shows a meeting house, and two and a half acres where the present church is located.

By 1813 a new brick church was under construction and at the 1818 Diocesan Convention, Bishop Moore reported that the large congregation at the mountain church was higher than the small number in Martinsburg.

The construction of the church was made possible by the generosity of Raleigh Colston, William Preston, and Josiah Hedges who gave the land and boarded the laborers during its construction.

During the Civil War, Rev. W. D. Hanson

conducted services at the church and ministered to all faiths & denominations during those troubled times. It was not used for any military purposes during that time due to the quick thinking of Rev. Hanson.

St Marks Methodist Episcopal Church "The Old Brick Church"

The church was built in 1839 of handmade bricks from the rich clay soil nearby. In the early settlement of the village, in 1836 Mary Claycomb sold for $17 half of lot No. 7 to the trustees of the Methodist Episcopal Church of the United States of America. For the next 27 years it was the Methodist Church in the town but in 1865 there was a split in the congregation that mirrored that of the area and the country as a whole. The congregation "locked out" those who favored slavery. There was a division in the Methodist Church of those who favored slavery and those who did not. St. Mark's became a Northern sympathizer congregation and in 1865-66, the Southern sympathizers built a log church building on what was Josiah Hedges development.

In what can be seen as evidence today, the

slave balcony was ripped out and the outside door bricked in so that the symbol of slavery was altered in the building. There was local lore that the church was used as a place to treat wounded soldiers during the Civil War but it cannot be substantiated. Being situated so close to the Town Spring area, that story can easily be believed.

It was not until 1942 that the North & South Methodist Churches reunited. After the merger, the larger Southern church building remained the Worship Center. On October 24, 1946 the building was sold to Edward & Dorothy Hull. In what is a rare move, the sale included the little cemetery that adjoins the church lot. The tombstones list deaths there in 1816 so there may have been another church structure on the lot. Ten days later the Hulls sold it to the Church of the Brethren denomination. It was used for a year and then it sat idle. In Nov. 1955, Alonzo D. Naylor purchased the "Old Brick Church" and presented it to the town. June Poisal got together a steering committee and established a library for the community. It continued as such until the new one was built in 2014.

The Hedgesville United Methodist Church - The building was constructed in 1866 of log. At one time it was the largest log structure still standing in Berkeley County. The southern sympathizers grouped together after being dismissed from the former Methodist Church; this mirrored what had happened to the Methodist denomination.

There were Presbyterians in the town who did not wish to journey to Spring Mills or to Back Creek Valley to attend services and so they joined with the Methodist to construct a church. A new Methodist Episcopal Church South was constructed on land donated by William H. Rickard. Up until 1893 this arrangement worked with two congregations but it was always known as a Methodist Church.

In the early 1922 the building was covered with stucco and the log appearance was masked.

HEDGESVILLE PRESBYTERIAN CHURCH

The church was constructed in 1894 as a chapel of the Falling Waters Presbyterian Church at Spring Mills .... Even though most of the congregation attended church at the Southern Methodist building. By 1892 some strains developed in the relationship and Hedgesville folks were encouraged to attend services at Spring Mills. The change was not well received so the Falling Waters session came up with a challenge... build your own chapel and we will provide preaching every two weeks. It was done. The group established a building committee started collecting money and borrowed some funds from a former confederate army veteran and within a short period of time, work was under way.

George W. Appel took a year to construct a New England style clapboard structure that perfect fit in with the emerging American Gothic period. Inside he devised a unique style of geometric wood designs that were symbols of the Trinity, Jesus, and the Gospels. Mr. Appel also built the pulpit for the Mt. Zion Episcopal Church in 1894.

In 1932, the congregation desired to be more than a chapel and in August 29, 1932 they were commissioned as a separate church.

METHODIST EPISCOPAL CHURCH – COLORED –[Article in Schools Section]

HEDGESVILLE & THE CIVIL WAR (A BRIEF GLIMPSE)

The Town of Hedgesville in the 1860's held four items that were of strategic importance during that time of our history that some still refer to as the War of the Rebellion.

The village came about because of its natural gap in the North Mountain allowing passage to the West. Within this gap was a natural limestone spring needed by both men and beast. A mile away to the north was the main line of the Baltimore & Ohio Railroad with its telegraph station for the speedy transmission of messages to Washington, D.C.

So it was all there --- a mountain that commanded a view of the Shenandoah Valley, a spring of never failing water, a natural gap in a near fifty mile mountain range, and a railroad. Each played its combined part to witness the service of men in gray and blue uniforms, as thousands of men with weapons of destruction swirled around the village.
All of these created problems and struggles

for inhabitants of the town.

We hope to give a broad overview of military actions near Hedgesville and then some specific instances of local families, but leave the more scholarly treatise to other local authors who have written from source material and are far more detailed.

There were five (5) major military operations in the county and four of them involved the Town in some manner.

1. Battle of Falling Waters (Hainesville) now Spring Mills on July 18, 1861

2. Destruction of Dam # 5 - December, 1861

3. General Bank's retreat through the county from Winchester, Virginia May 25, 1862

4. Stonewall Jackson's control of Martinsburg - September, 1862

5. Chambersburg Raid by J. E. B. Stuart - October 9, 1862

The Town itself changed hands from Confederate to Union many times depending upon the need of the army unit in proximity at the moment. It was told that the Union troops once threatened to burn the down when they found they could not hold it. The townspeople did not have time to evacuate their homes or belongings so they put on several layers of garments and fled to the mountains. When they returned the next morning, they found that nothing had been damaged.

Much recruiting was done in the town by both sides. The recruiting was usually done at Bodine Tavern near the town spring. It was reported that when reasoning failed, the army would shanghai people, gather up drunks, or promise able-bodied men that they would be officers.

Several houses in Hedgesville housed soldiers during the war. In fact, any large house was pressed into service, whether the owner agreed to the arrangements or not. A house that stood near the town spring, the Gabriel House, was a hostelry.

There was an incident involving one of the town's doctors.

Dr. Buckles received a request to go to McCoy's Ferry to treat someone who was ill. He stayed late and apparently "hit the cider barrel" before returning. He was almost shot by a soldier who was on guard (picket) duty at the school house hill. Apparently Dr. Buckles rode on after being told to halt.

When J.E.B. Stuart was on his way to plunder Chambersburg, Pa he came by way of the gap in the mountain. He sealed off the Town of Hedgesville so no one could spread the word of his movements. He issued passes to go in or out of the village and this may have been the incident.

There was a company of soldiers organized before the Civil War. They were known as the Home Guards or the Virginia Militia and they met at Bodines at the town spring. They practiced their drills around the spring area and "downed a few" at the tavern.

Captain W. B. Colston near what is now Honeywood, lived in a house called" Medway." Captain Colson wrote extensively of his experiences in the Civil War and Co. E. - "The Hedgesville Blues"

"Hostilities may be said to date from the John Brown raid. Brown chose Harpers Ferry as the scene of his operation. The south was thoroughly aroused by this dastardly act and realized that the war with the north was inevitable, and in preparation for the coming struggles, set about organizing military companies in every county, south of the Potomac River. In Berkeley County, there were four companies raised --- two infantry, one cavalry, and one artillery. My brother Raleigh T. Colston, who had been educated at the Virginia Military Institute, enlisted one of those infantry companies in the vicinity of Hedgesville, of which he was made Captain and I was a private in the same company.

We used to meet twice a week for drill and instruction, sometimes in the afternoon, and sometimes at night.

I remember one night we got home from drill about 11 o'clock and as we were coming from the stable to the house, our attention was attracted by a bright light in the sky. I remarked that I believed it was at Harpers Ferry, where the United States had an armory and a large number of arms and ammunition stored. Raleigh did not agree with me and went to bed, but had not been there long before we heard a call under our window and upon inquiry found that a messenger had been sent from Martinsburg with an order from General Richardson, who was in command of the militia, to Raleigh to call out his troops and report to Harpers Ferry as soon as possible. There was no more sleep for us that night. Virginia had passed the ordinance of secession (April 17, 1861) and we knew that the tug of war had come, but little did we realize the deadly struggle that was before us.

As soon as day began to break, Raleigh and I mounted our horses and started with speed, in opposite directions, to notify the members of the company to repair to the headquarters in Hedgesville. By nine o'clock we had them all assembled and marched to North Mountain Station on the B & O railroad to take a train to Harpers Ferry, where we found the other Berkeley County companies "

HEDGESVILLE BLUES COMPANY E, SECOND REGIMENT VIRGINIA INFANTRY, BERKELEY COUNTY CONFEDERATE STATES ARMY (Original Roster)

The company was organized in the fall of 1859, in the Town of Hedgesville and vicinity, immediately after the John Brown Raid, when the Southern people became impressed with the idea that their institutions were menaced by Northern fanatics. Mr. M. C. Nadenbousch was its first Captain and Raleigh T. Colston, who attended Virginia Military Institute, was First Lieutenant. Captain Colston was ordered to report with his company to Harpers Ferry when the war cloud burst. Company E was assigned to the 2nd Virginia Regiment which formed a part of the famous "Stonewall Brigade" and participated in all of the battles in which that gallant corps was engaged. They ended the war at Appomattox with the final surrender by General Lee.

The following is a short military biographical sketch of the group:

Name
Age When Enlisted

Raleigh T. Colson
27

He was born Feb. 18, 1834 at the Honeywood Estate. After Mr. M. C. Nadenbousch resigned having had no military training, the command fell to Raleigh. Cited for gallantry at First Manassas, he lead the expedition against Dam No. 5 locally. He fought also at Second Manassas. He was second in command at Fredericksburg; fought at Chancellorsville & Gettysburg. Seriously wounded in the leg at the Mine Run Campaign, he was removed from the battlefield. His leg had to be amputated at a field hospital. While waiting in the rain at the Orange County Court House for an ambulance to take him to Charlottesville, he contracted pneumonia and died. He is buried at the cemetery of the University of Charlottesville.

David H. Manor
22

A millwright who was born Jan. 19, 1839 He enlisted April 19, 1861 at Hedgesville in Co. E. He was killed in action at First Manassas on July 21, 1861 and is buried at the Hedgesville Cemetery

Aaron H. Myers
22

A farmer who enlisted in Company E on April 19, 1861 at Hedgesville

Cromwell L. Myers
26

A tinner who listed his birth on Feb. 7, 1835 and enlisted on April 19, 1861 in Hedgesville. He was taken prisoner at Kernstown March 23, 1862 but gained his freedom by a prisoner exchange on August 5, 1862. He died October 24, 18__ and is buried In the Hedgesville Cemetery.

W. B. Colston
25

A brother to Raleigh T. Colson, he became a private in the same company. He fought in all of the same battles as his brother. He was wounded and discovered by Raleigh. He was taken to the field hospital at Middletown that was in a church. His left leg was paralyzed.

John T. Hull
22

Like his father, he was a carpenter in Hedgesville. He enlisted April 19, 1861 at that place. He was wounded at Port Republic and on May 8, 1863 was wounded in the neck at Chancellorsville. He returned to live in Hedgesville at the Summit House and is buried in the Hedgesville Cemetery.

Allen Wandling
25

A miller who was born on May 7, 1836 and enlisted in the Hedesville Blues He is buried at the Hedgesville Cemetery.

Issac N. Bayne
19

Possibly born in 1842 who listed himself as

a carpenter when he joined at Hedgesville on April 19, 1861 He had noted in his records that he had fair complexion, grey eyes, and dark hair. He was wounded at Chancellorsville and moved to a hospital in Richmond, Staunton, and then Lynchburg.

Jacob Deck
21

A merchant who likewise enlisted April 19, 1861 in Hedgesville

George T. Kreglow
22

A farmer who gave his birth date as Jan. 20, 1839 when he enlisted with the others on April 18, 1861 He is buried in the Hedgesville Cemetery.

Emmanuel Basore
24

Born in 1837? His occupation was listed as carpenter. He is listed as "present" from April 6, 1861 to May, 1862 when he was taken ill. He was sent to Chimborazo

Hospital from May 3-16. He then rejoined the company and served until November, when he was detached by Gen. Jackson to report to Captain Nadenbousch for recruiting duty. He returned to the company in December.

George Claiborne
25

A cooper who enlisted April 19, 1861 in Co. E as a private

William L. Cunningham
25
Born Feb 14, 1836, he gave his occupation as a farmer when he enlisted April 19, 1861 He is buried at Falling Waters Cemetery at Spring Mills.

Joseph N. Davis
25

A shoemaker who enlisted April 19, 1861 as a private in Co. E

James W. Dugan
21?

A farmer who enlisted in Hedgesville on April 19, 1861 He was taken a prisoner of war at Kernstown on March 23, 1862 and taken to Ft. Delaware; exchanged Aug 5, 1862, he was wounded in the hand at Second Manassas. He was wounded again at Chancellorsville. He was discharged as totally disqualified on September 22, 1864.

Issac H. Eversole
20
A farmer listed as 5'8" with fair complexion, blue eyes, light hair
He enlisted April 19, 1861 at Hedgesville. He came to be a prisoner of war at Winchester but was exchanged March 28, 1863.

Jacob T. Eversole
18

A farmer who enlisted with the main group on April 19, 1861 in Hedgesville He was wounded at Winchester an discharged on Dec. 4, 1862. He is buried at the Cemetery in Little Georgetown.

John Wm. Eversole
29

A farmer who enlisted April 19, 1861. He died in 1912 and is buried in the Hedgesville Cemetery.

James Fiery
30

A cooper who enlisted with the group April, 1861 He received a gunshot wound resulting in a compound fracture of the right leg. He died May 26, 1864 at Charlottesville.

John Wm. Guinn
19

Enlisted April 19, 1861 at Hedgesville as a Private

George Hull
23

Born 1835 He was 5'5" tall with light complexion, hazel eyes, and brown hair when he enlisted with the main body on April 19, 1861. He was a carpenter. He was wounded in foot at Payne's Farm. He became a prisoner of war near Petersburg.

William Jordon
23

A farmer who enlisted April 19, 1861 in Co. E. as a private

John W. Joy
24

Born in 1815 or there about; he listed his occupation as farmer. Enlisted as a private in Hedgesville on April 19, 1861

Issac Keesecker
20
A shoemaker who enlisted with the main group in April 19, 1861
He was wounded at Cedar Mountain and later died at Mt. Jackson, VA on December 16, 1864.

Walter Hedges Lingamfelter
31

He listed himself as a farmer who enlisted with the larger group. He was wounded in the head at Monocracy on July 9, 1864; later he became a prisoner of war at Frederick, MD. He was taken to the Old Capitol Prison, exchanged for a Union soldier but later had the misfortune of being captured and again became a prisoner of War near Petersburg, VA. He died April 13, 1901 and is buried at the Hedgesville Cemetery.

Charles W. Manor
24

A millwright who described himself as having a dark complexion, grey eyes, and dark hair He was wounded in the face at First Manassas, wounded the second time at Malvern Hill, and wounded the third time in the right thigh and left leg. He was captured and became a prisoner of war at Cedar Creek but was exchanged and given a furlough. He died October 5, 1908 and is buried in the Hedgesville Cemetery.

George W. Miller
20

Enlisted April 19, 1861 at Hedgesville as a private He was wounded at First Manassas. Some records show that he went AWOL, sentenced to a court martial, then became ill, and subsequently sentenced to hard labor. He was admitted to a hospital for a cut toe in North Carolina in 1865. He died in 1917 and is buried at Port Republic, VA .

Harvey A. Miller
26

A farmer who enlisted as one of the group on April 19, 1861
He fought with Company E but later transferred to the cavalry. He died on Nov. 8, 1902 and is buried at Falling Waters Cemetery.

Cromwell L. Meyers
26

A farmer from Hedgesville, he enlisted as part of the group on April 19, 1861.

George T. Sperow
19

A plasterer who enlisted as above on April 19, 1861 He died in 1904 and is buried in Elmwood Cemetery in Shepherdstown, WV.

Charles Sutton
23

A carpenter who enlisted with the main group on April 19, 1861

Michael White
29

A carpenter who enlisted with the main group on April 19, 1861

ADDITIONAL LISTINGS

These men just listed are the original group that comprised Company "E"; however, other men enlisted at other times and other places during the war. Here is an attempt to chronicle some of them that are of interest to this Hedgesville area.

John T. Bodine
?

A farmer who stated he was born July 24, 1839 who enlisted with the original group but not listed as being one of the original group? He is buried in the Hedgesville Cemetery.

James M. V. B. Guinn
19

When he enlisted in Harpers Ferry on April 21, 1861 he was a shoemaker. His description was given as having grey eyes, black hair, 5'9" tall with light complexion. Later He was listed as being ill with rheumatism, then AWOL , captured by the enemy and was exchanged. He died Nov. 23, 1906 and is buried in the Hedgesville Cemetery.

Theodore Hedges
18

He was drafted at Bunker Hill in Co. E. Some sources say he may have served in the Calvary. He is buried in the Hedgesville Cemetery.

Dallas Hull
18

From Hedgesville, but enlisted at Winchester. His description is given as having light hair, hazel eyes, 5'7" tall, with light complexion. He was wounded in the ankle at Paynes Farm. He died October 31, 1911 at the Soldiers Home in Richmond, VA. He is buried in the Hedgesville Cemetery.

Jeremiah Lanham
18

A farmer who when he enlisted was reported to be 5'6" tall, having black hair and hazel eyes. He enlisted at Harpers Ferry. Absent on several occasions, tried and acquitted by court martial, he was captured by the enemy during the retreat from Gettysburg.

Jacob Lewis
26

A farmer from Berkeley County who enlisted at Winchester He was arrested by Union troops in Berkeley County and sent to prison in Wheeling. He was later exchanged. He is buried in Charles Town, WV.

William H. Light
?

Possibly an engineer, he was wounded in the face and neck at First Manassas. **He was one of the 14 men remaining who surrendered at Appomattox to conclude the war.**

John & G. B. Lindamood

?

Both enlisted at Rude'Hill and were **among the 14 who surrendered at Appamattox.**

Issac Merchant

24

Enlisted at Bunker Hill on October 4, 1862, wounded at Chancellorsville, captured at Fort Steadman near Petersburg and is buried in Arlington National Cemetery.

Michael O'Connor or *Conner*

Wounded in the left shoulder, he was wounded again at Cedar Mountain, and then wounded a third time at Petersburg. He was **one of the 14 who surrendered at Appomattox**. He is buried at St. Joseph Cemetery in Martinsburg, WV

Thomas Payne

?

He enlisted April 16, 1862 in Winchester, VA. He is buried at the Falling Waters Cemetery at Spring Mills.

William R. Peregoy
18

He enlisted October 4, 1862 at Bunker Hill. He surrendered as **one of the 14 from Company E at Appomattox.** He died in 1926 and is buried in Harpers Ferry.

Frances H. Pike ?

He enlisted at Winchester but became a prisoner of war of the enemy at Kernstown nearby. He was exchanged but later wounded in the lung in combat at Second Manassas**. He surrendered as one of the 14 from Co E at Appamattox.**

Jacob Poisal
?

He enlisted at Bunker Hill on October 4, 1862. He lived in Hedgesville for a while after the war but is not buried in the Hedgesville Cemetery.

Charles Porterfield
?
He enlisted at Bunker Hill on October 4, 1862. He was wounded by a shell at Fredericksburg. Later for losing his gun, he was assessed $36 in pay.

Jacob Porterfield ?

Enlisted October 4, 1862 at Bunker Hill

John Pryor
19
A stone mason who enlisted June 20, 1861 in Martinsburg He was captured by the enemy at Kernstown, wounded at Second Manassas, and captured during the retreat from Gettysburg. He is buried at St. Joseph Cemetery in Martinsburg, WV.

John Riddle
18
He enlisted at Darkesville July 10, 1863. He was killed in action near New Market, VA and is buried at Norborne Cemetery in Martinsburg.

George F. Rockwell
?

He enlisted March, 1862 at Winchester, VA. At one time he was a commander of the group. He left service on April 25, 1865 at the end of the war.

John M. Small
23

He enlisted March 26, 1862 and given detail as a teamster. He was **one of the 14 to surrender at Appomattox.** He is buried in the Greenhill Cemetery in Martinsburg.

Reuben M. Small
26
He enlisted March 26, 1862. He became a tactical musician for the 2nd regiment. **He was one of the 14 to surrender at Appomattox.**

A Porterfield Snodgrass
17

One of the youngest of the troops, he enlisted July 15, 1863. His description is given as being 5'10" tall, light hair, and grey eyes. He was wounded in the leg at Paynes Farm near Farmville, VA. He died Dec. 9, 1895 and is buried in Greenhill Cemetery in Martinsburg.

John W. Stuckey
?

He enlisted April 24, 1863 at Swift Run Gap. He was killed in action August 29, 1862 at Second Manassas.

Samuel A. Stuckey
19

A farmer who enlisted April 24, 1862 at Swift Run Gap He was wounded at Fredericksburg. He was captured near Back Creek on July 12, 1864 and sent to Wheeling Prison but was exchanged on March 7, 1865.

Edward Tobin
23

A stone mason who enlisted at Harpers Ferry May 5, 1861. He was not listed on the rolls by July 31, 1861.

George W. Weddle
?

He enlisted in Winchester, but he was from Berkeley County, on March 4, 1862. He was wounded in the hip at Port Republic. He **was one of the 14 who surrendered at Appomattox.**

John G. Whitmore
23
He is described as having light complexion, dark hair, blue eyes
His residence was Rockingham County, VA. On Jan 15, 1864 he was captured and sent north. He died July 7, 1906 and is buried at Falling Waters Cemetery at Spring Mills.
[These *are not the only names of men who fought for the Confederates in the area, but just the names of one Company of soldiers – Company E who were originally formed in Hedgesville and of their original roster]*

A FAMILY EXODUS FROM HEDGESVILLE

Alfred Hamilton Windham was a cooper (barrel maker) and blacksmith at Hedgesville from approximately 1839 to 1860. He operated his own blacksmith shop and had a thriving business. He attended the Northern Methodist Church in the town. When the

Civil War came early to the area and bullets were flying near his blacksmith shop, he decided to leave the area. Alfred's slaves pleaded in vain to accompany him. Prior to leaving he was required to pay $1,000 each for "substitute soldiers" for military service for himself and his two oldest sons, Thomas & James. Incidents were recorded that describe Alfred, wife Nancy, and their eight children's trip to Logan County, Ohio which began April 1, 1861 and ended May 5, 1861. The first bridge they crossed after leaving Hedgesville was destroyed soon after they got over it. The family traveled by covered wagon, possibly two wagons, since they had two, four horse teams to transport ten people and equipment. They encountered spring rains which made trails muddy and caused frequent "bog downs." The family was encamped for the night near a mountain "inn." Army officers rode up and demanded some of their horses; horses were in demand by both armies at the time. The inn-keeper interceded and convinced the officers that all eight horses were needed to get the family to Ohio.

Upon arrival at their new home, Alfred exchanged some of the horses for oxen which were used to clear the land. He became a farmer but continued to do blacksmith work in a small shop behind his house.

THE BATTLE OF NORTH MOUNTAIN DEPOT

On the morning of July 3, 1864, Brigadier General McCausland sent his Virginia Cavalry brigade against two companies of the 135th Ohio Infantry manning a two-story blockhouse near the railroad crossing at North Mountain Depot. After a spirited fight, the Ohioans finally surrendered when McCausland's artillery arrived and opened up on their fortifications. The casualties were light on both sides.

The Confederates sent their captives to prison camps in the deep South. Over the next year, 90 of the 163 soldiers taken prisoner died of disease contracted while in prison.

TOWARD THE NEW CENTURY

The area of Berkeley County was devastated after the war. The heavy utilization of all natural resources by opposing armies, the deprivation of the local citizens who had been stripped of crops and animals on the farms, and the lack of commerce had just depleted the area.

Fortunately there was the B & O Railroad which continued to haul goods and services to the area. Along with the early munificence of the Federal government at Washington who sought to reconstruct the area, allowed an opportunity for people to "get back on their feet" and become economically viable again.

By 1873, eight years after the Civil War was over, the village of Hedgesville had been able to return to some form of normalcy. There were veterans living in the town and some in the cemetery but that was secondary to establishing life again.

Here are excerpts from CHRONICLES OF OLD BERKELEY, a book by Hedgesville native Ann

Henshaw Gardiner who quotes the town minute book:

"By 1873, the tax levy in Hedgesville was fifteen cents on the hundred dollars. At a council meeting on May 12, 1873 - On the motion the Street Supervisor, Joel Paregoy, to be instructed to see Mr. H. W. Rickard in regard to whitewashing the town spring house and if he does not get it done to have it down himself. And get the top covered with tin; also to do the work that he thinks is necessary to be done about the Spring and watering place. Motion carried.

On June 5, 1873, The Council passed a motion to pay a bill presented to G. Wynkoop for latches for the Town Spring House amounting to 30 cents.

A motion passed the Council June 16, 1873, that the Street Supervisor be instructed to procure an Iron Dipper for use at the Town Spring. The levy was increased to 30 cents on the hundred dollars but in a meeting on June 1, 1874 was reduced to fifteen cents on the hundred dollars.

On April 30, 1875, on motion by Jacob Naylor a law be made allowing no stone throwing, snow balling, or ball playing in the incorporation [town] limits.

The following was offered as a by-law, accepted and passed unanimously to go into effect Monday, May 3, 1875:

Be it enacted, that if any person or persons be guilty of throwing stones or other missile, playing ball or snow balling within the Corporation, the same shall be fined not less than one or more than five dollars, also further, be it enacted, that if any person or person be guilty of trespassing on any person's property (such as houses, lots, trees, and gardens) they shall be deal with in accordance with the same provisions of the above section. .

The Council at its May 25, 1875, received the following fee for a license. "The Mayor reports one dollar received from a peddler for a license for three months to see if he can sell goods in the corporation of Hedgesville commencing the 5th day of May 1875 and ending the 5th day of August 1875. The treasurer received the money.

On June 1, 1875, the Council made the levy ten cents on the hundred dollars for the

year. At a meeting on Tuesday, August 7, 1875, On motion made by Jacob Naylor and seconded by William Shaffer that Mr. Poisal be instructed to employ boys to pull weeds out of the streets and alleys, price not to exceed five cents an hour. Bill rendered by Michael Poisal for pulling weeds in the streets and alley ways was $8.37. Ordered paid.
The town along with all others had the long struggle over the question of "Hogs in or Hogs Out debate." After several meetings it was finally decided that hogs could stay but penned up and attended to by their owners.

The Council declared on Christmas Day - Dec. 25, 1875, "All fireworks is a nusens" and passed the following act: "Be it enacted, that no fireworks, crackers, squibs, torpedoes, etc. shall be sold within the town limits from ½ past three o'clock, Dec. 25, 1875. Any party violating the same shall be fined by the Mayor not less than five no more than ten dollars for every violation. Motion carried.

One constant and troublesome question before the Council was the request for license to sell spirituous liquors in the town... in most instances these requests were refused....

The hogs might be safe to be in the town limits... but now it was ducks who were in question.

"On April 17, 1877, the Council passed the following ordinance: Be it enacted by the Council of the Corporation of Hedgesville, there shall be no ducks nor geese allowed to run at large in the limits of the town. Any person or persons so allowing their poultry of this species offending against said such ordinance shall be subject to a fine not less than two nor more than five dollars for every offense, and in default of payment of said fine, the poultry will be taken by the Corporation authority to satisfy such fines as may be imposed. All former enactments in reference to the poultry specified is hereby amended. Motion carried."

The need came for lights to light the streets and alley ways and the Council acted after thirty petitioners spoke:

The Council in its meeting on May 25, 1891, "upon the petition of thirty tax payers asking for street lamps," authorized the Mayor to purchase six lamps to be placed at different sections of the town. The Council provided an oil can and a spigot for the oil barrel, and a ladder for the lamp lighter. The lamp lighter's contract provided … the lamps be lit not less than 17 nights nor more than 20 in one month; that the globes be cleaned twice a week, the wicks be kept properly trimmed, and that the Can be filled with oil every day. The lamps were to be out 10 ½ o'clock in the summer and nine ½ o'clock in winter time….. "

The Martinsburg Herald on Saturday, July 6, 1889 printed this article about Hedgesville which promotes the thriving town:

"Hedgesville is located in a gap of the North Mountain, 7 miles west of Martinsburg the County Seat, and 1 mile from North Mountain Station on the B & O Railroad.

There is every facility here for manufacturing of various kinds. For health & scenery our village can't be surpassed. There is not a village in the state that can boast of as fine a water, we have hard or soft, in addition, within ½ mile of the village, just a walk, we have the finest iron and chalybeate water, so the reader will see at a glance we have one of the most requisite essentials of health.

The mortality for the last 12 months of the village of a population of 400 has only reached 3, less than 1/4th of one percent of the population.

As to scenery we have two fine elevations easy to ascend overlooking a fine and fertile Valley East that you can see as far as the eye can carry. Williamsport, Clear Spring, Pen Mar, Fort Frederick, and the outskirts of Hagerstown and Martinsburg can easily be seen without the aid of a telescope.

As to churches. First is the Episcopal, the oldest in the village, the rector is Rev. W. T. Leavel, a native of Jefferson County, who for his age is an active worker in church work, a plain, earnest and practical preacher. Second, is the Methodist Episcopal built in 1836 under the administration of Rev. Berkeley. The church was included in the Berkeley Circuit and Martinsburg at that time was one of the charges of the circuit. The present pastor is the Rev. Seibert, a young man, an able and earnest worker. Third, is the M. E. Church, South, which is presided over by the Rev. Snapp, quite unassuming in his manner though a sound and logical talker. Fourth, is the M. E. Church, Colored, which is quite a neat and attractive structure, the present pastor is Rev. Lane. Rev. H. Gilmore of the Presbyterian Church preaches in the M. E. Church, South, every two weeks at night; he is highly esteemed by all denominations.

As to doctors we have a full supply; Drs. G. S. Hanna, C.L. Mitchell, Drs Harris & Hess. We have an able faculty of Medical men as there is in the county.

Our school building is a large and commodious structure built of brick, divided into 4 rooms; our school board is W. H. Kilmer, President - T. Siler, and Abram Van meter, commissioners Trustees are M.C. Nadenbousch, Seibert Speck, and Dr. Hess.

John H. Miller is our oldest merchant; he commenced business here during the War, and by his strict attention to business has been quite successful and accumulated a considerable amount of property.
E. P. Beall comes next, a native of Maryland, has built up a fine trade and made money. J. S. Vermilyea, a native of the town commenced business here as a confectioner also during the war and he is still adding to

his business. At the present time he keeps a general line of merchandise, also furnishes the principal portion of coal that is used; in addition to his store, he carries on his farm and is considered one of the most practical farmers we have.

Lee Lingamfelter keeps a full line of confection goods and a tin store. Jacob Chapman keeps a notion store where the ladies will always find a nice line of trimmings such as ribbons, lace, silks, collars, etc. We have 3 Milliner shops:

M. E. Gaff, Mrs. M. F. Poisal, and Miss Blanche Smaltz.

J. T. Slaughter and George Apple are our carpenters and both first class workman as you will find in the county. Cabinet makers and undertakers are A. J. Jacques and C. M. Brown; both have as fine hearses as there are in the county. Mr. Brown keeps on hand a fine supply of caskets, etc.

Mr. A. H. Brown, butcher, is ready at all times to furnish the best of meats. He has a life-time experience in the business. J. C. Heberlig and Charles Grabill are engaged in the lumber business and ready at all times to furnish lumber for building purposes. Mr. Heberlig carries on the business extensively, has 4 mills and ships lumber to Europe. Mr. Way and Snyder are Plasterers. George W. Snyder are painters and are good workman and reasonable in their charges.

Dr. M. S. Butler, a doctor and a druggist, keeps on hand a full and well selected stock of drugs, medicines, paints, oil and in fact, everything that is kept in a first class drug store.

J. H. Morrow, Jeweler, keeps on hand a good stock in his line an does all kind of repairing in his business in first class style. Edward Morrow is a harness maker. J. W. Guinn attends to the soles of the people, that is the soles of their feet. John understands the business and will give you a good fit. Jacob Naylor, Blacksmith, is ready all the time to build your wagons and do repairs in that line. Mr. Edgar Henshaw, is Post Master and Roland Hanna is his assistant
Jacob Harrison, Merchant Tailor, keeps on hand a good and well selected stock of goods at moderate prices.

The Council officers are: Mayor, J.S. Vermilyea, and Council members, Dr. M. S. Butler, C. Grabill, Hamilton Myers, J. C. Heberlig and W. Rickard.

The Summit House is kept by Mr. Jacob Hull one of the oldest citizens of the town. The trading public will always find his table well furnished and the prices moderate.

Among our most enterprising farmers are C. Joys, Dr. W. Lemon, John Felker, Wm. Lingamfelter, Sibert Speck, George Rineman which list their post office at Hedgesville. Other farmers who list their post office at North Mountain are:
C. K. Robbins, Allen Robbins, J. R. Criswell, Lemuel Dirting, Peter Sperow, Charles Donaldson, William Kilmer and Jno. Rickard.

SCHOOLS IN HEDGESVILLE

By 1820 there were only two houses in the town and the Mt. Zion Episcopal Church but by the 1830's and 1840's there were other houses being built to comprise a village. It was time to think of education and school buildings and indeed the Town of Hedgesville has been known for being an educational center since its inception.

Robert S. Snodgrass of Snodgrass Tavern had been elected to the Virginia legislature meeting at Richmond and he wrote to his wife, Sarah Snodgrass, on January 15, 1839 .... " Tell the children I want them to learn as much as they can, so they will be able to go to the Hedgesville School in the Spring. "

These were "private" schools in the sense that there were no "public" schools. They began with a few families banding together to hire a teacher for a prescribed number of weeks.

The teacher would "board" with one of the families and the school would be held at the family home. Later a school house would be established and open to those families who would share the cost.

In the area, it is known that a log school house had been erected on the Harland land just above Harlan Springs which seems to have been in operation from 1836-1860. At this time the school had as many as three teachers on the faculty. The Rev. Lewis F. Wilson of the Presbyterian Church, Hunter Harlan, and Hillary Herbert were known to have been teachers in the school.

Another private school was conducted by the Rev. Lewis Wilson at his home at Cumbo after he built there in 1840. After he moved to Hedgesville in 1845, he continued the school at Hedgesville in his home.

According to an old diary of the time there was in 1854, a boarding school for little children conducted by a Mrs. Johnston. It was located in what is known as the Ronk-Tabler house on Main Street and was known as Summit Hall; it was still in operation by 1885.

Across the street from this school was another private school conducted by a Mrs. Smith and her daughter. It was located in a building at the back of the property which later became a barn.

There is no supporting evidence but Mr. R. A. Jacques made mention that when he was a boy there were two schools in the village - one for the boys at the North Mountain road and one for the girls on the opposite side.

The site of the Mt. Lebanon-Methodist-Episcopal (colored) Church on the opposite side of the mountain range was first built as a school. A private school, Pleasant Hill School, had been there before but it had burned. The "new" public school had been built of brick on the opposite knoll of the village in 1884.

In 1866, free schools were introduced in West Virginia. Mr. J. H. Alexandria was the first one who taught in the white school under the free school system and Miss Laura Harley was the second teacher there. And from a school it turned into a church in 1887.

Somewhere along in time a public *elementary* school was established on its own and Mr. C. W. Keesecker was the first Principal according to records. He quit public education to take a job delivering the mail for more money. Miss Jane Riner succeeded him as the Head Teacher. She went to another school and Mr. Charles Stuckey assumed the position of Principal until he retired in 1959.

According to teacher registers required yearly, in 1897, the elementary school had developed into a high school. These are the listing of the Principals from those records:

1884-1893 T. H. Cox
1893-1897 Edgar Bowers
1877-1902 J. C. Sanders
1902-1903 Mary Sanders
1903-1904 H. C. Coe
1904-1908 Walter Duke - left to become a teacher at Shepherd College
1908-1910 Robert Bates
1910-1923 F. M. Miller

It was told that previous to Mr. Miller coming to Hedgesville, the school had become a full fledged high school but less than first class. Mr. Miller began to build up the school. He had help from the West Virginia State Department of Education and they worked out a proper curriculum and obtained the proper qualified teachers to teach its parts. In due course, the high school had reached its academic standing and was ranked ahead of Martinsburg who had much more in the way of economic resources. The first graduating class was held in 1910.

1923-1925 Harry Stuckey
1925-1926 Ralph Rice
1927–1930 A. L. Rodgers

The building of the new high school was a tremendous undertaking for the people of Hedgesville. In those days each magisterial district had its own school system with Board of Education, schools, and teachers. The taxes from that particular magisterial district supported the schools so it did not appear there was any way that Hedgesville could erect a new school with the limited property base that it had.

Dr. Daniel Reed Ross and his family lived in Hedgesville. In addition to being a physician, surgeon, dentist, etc. he was active in local affairs. He was politically inclined and took a great interest in the schools of the district. It is said that it was due to Dr. Ross realization that the Baltimore & Ohio Railroad which crossed the Hedgesville District, was not paying the amount of taxes which were thought to be appropriate for a corporation of that size & magnitude. It was due to his efforts that the situation was remedied with the result that the Hedgesville School District became immensely prosperous and was able to increase the size of its teaching staff and the quality of the teaching staff especially the high school.

They decided to build a new high school building on the spot that the old school had been located. The building had been condemned because it was so rickety that the top floors could not be used when the wind blew very hard.

The Board of Education then looked for a place where they could hold school while there was the transition of building from the old to the new. There was only one building close that could accommodate the students and they decided to rent the Mt. Clifton Hotel for a year and use its spacious rooms for classrooms. It was strange but there was a graduating class that graduated from that building and the only one to graduate from a hotel.

[Further in the book there will be a section devoted to the Hotel itself]

1930-1931 Kenneth Meyers

1931-1933 F. X. Creedle
1933-1945 George P. Ludwig

Mr. Ludwig wrote the school song which is still in use today. The music is patterned after a hymn but the words are original. Another stanza was added during World War II to reflect the patriotic times but it has never been altered. Mr. Ludwig came back to Hedgesville High School and finished his education career as a Social Studies teacher retiring in 1959.

1945-1949 F. M. Miller came back and retired from the position.

1949-1956 Charles Lord went on to become a college professor of History at Millersville State College in Pennsylvania

1956-1984 Robert D. Kilmer - to the building of second new high school 1976 and beyond. a local man, he was a former coach, teacher, and student at Hedgesville High School. Robert Kilmer was longest serving principal, serving 28 years with the school being in two locations!

In the 1950's enrollment had grown so large that it was not possible to house the elementary students on the lower floor of the high school and the secondary students on the top floor, so a new elementary school had to be constructed.

It was started in 1952 and two grades were moved down there with Miss June Poisal as the Head Teacher. After that two year period, the other elementary grades 3-6 were moved down to the new building. Charles L. Stuckey was the Principal there from 1945-1959. He said in a speech when he retired ... "After *41 years of regular teaching, and 12 years of substituting, I like the old song, I lay down the shovel and the hoe."* [Title of old Stephen Foster song]

Miss June Poisal became the Principal in 1959 and continued until 1972. She is known for having established a community library in Hedgesville, obtaining a building, Naylor Hall, for its use, helping to furnish it with books, supporting it financially and continued in its operation until she died.

Mr. David McClung succeeded Miss Poisal as the Principal.

Due to another population boom in the area, the school was reconfigured as a K-2. Another local person, Paul Tyson became principal and retired from that position.

DOCTORS IN HEDGESVILLE

At the turn of the century the little village was vibrant with people and commerce. There was need for medical care and several doctors came to practice in the town and surrounding areas.

Here are remembrances from people who recalled some of them:

Katherine Butler Heiskell:

"**Dr. Michael Seibert Butler** was an early physician and he was married to Lilly Snodgrass Henshaw of Bunker Hill. He came to practice in Hedgesville about 1875. I am his granddaughter.

One of my earliest memories was him going in a horse & buggy to different parts of the county to visit his patients. One day he would be in the Dam No. 5 area and then next he would be in Johnsontown. He would be in different parts of the area every day. When he was at home he would see patients regardless of what hour of the day or night and I can remember hearing pebbles or stones up against my window at maybe 2 o'clock in the morning. I would hear somebody say "Doc, it is time" and he would say, "Well I will be right down." He would go down and get one of his horses, put on a saddle and away they would go. He would turn no one down who sought his help.

He would come home with a bag of potatoes, sometime he would be given meat, sometimes even nothing but a promise to pay.

He used horses but along came the Ford and he had to learn to drive a car. This was quite difficult for him. He would manage alright on the country roads but sometimes the car would get stuck in the mud and he would have to wait until somebody came along to pull him out or he would walk to the nearest spot for help.

Another time, water at Back Creek was very, very high and he was needed across the other side. He tied a rope around his waist, the other end was tied to a tree on the other side, and he pulled himself across to the other bank.

He seemed to have problems with putting the car in the barn. When he got home, for some reason, when he was ready to turn to go through his yard to go to the barn/garage, he would step on the gas and he would go scooting through the yard and most always hit the back of the barn.

He also had to be his own pharmacist because he dispensed medicine.

I know he worked with Dr. T. K. Oates with surgical patients. People were afraid of operations; people didn't want them but after there was a hospital in Martinsburg in 1905, he was determined to try to get anybody who needed surgery to go to the hospital and have it done. Every year he would go down to Hopkins in Baltimore to study or do advanced courses.

In his house he would not let anybody touch a single, solitary thing in his office which was also the living room. We had a parlor but that was only for company. Patients and family were both in the living room. The table was piled up high and helter-skelter but you dare not touch any of it. He could put his hand on anything that he wanted but nobody else could touch anything.

He practiced medicine up until his death

which was in 1926. "
Sara Frye Poisal:

" I am the daughter of **Dr. David Paul Frye**. He was born in Middleway, WV in Jefferson County. When quite young he started reading medicine under Dr. George A. Davis of Middleway. He entered the College of Physicians & Surgeons in Baltimore from which he graduated in March, 1889 at the age of 21. He was granted a certificate to practice medicine in West Virginia that was signed by Dr. Newton D. Baker of Martinsburg, a member of the State Board of Health.

He located in Middleway and then moved 16 years later to Hedgesville where he resided at the time of his death in April 14, 1943.

He was a typical country doctor of the time. He drove a double team of horses over Berkeley & Morgan counties. When the weather was bad he rode on horseback and used saddle bags. He also went by train to Cherry Run and sometimes to Sleepy Creek when the roads were impassable.

About 1913 there was an epidemic of typhoid fever and he was very proud that he only lost one patient to the disease. He attributed that to the fact that they gave the patient food when he expressly told them not to. He was quite successful in the 1918 flu epidemic. He did not lose one patient and he was quite proud of that record.

During these epidemics he would often leave home at daylight and did not return until midnight or later. At meal time he ate wherever he happened to be and would feed his horses.

He was an ardent Democrat, a Mason, member of the Board of Education of Middleway, and a charter member of the Eastern Panhandle Medical Association.

Geraldine Ward LeMaster:

I was the eldest daughter of **Dr. E. A. Ward.** He came to Hedgesville in the spring of 1895 from Rio, West Virginia, where he had practiced medicine for a short time. He was born in Capon Bridge, West Virginia. He attended medical college in Virginia and did his intern work at John Hopkins Hospital in Baltimore, MD. He married Ella V. Oates of Capon Bridge in 1894.

He had a large practice in the Hedgesville area. Road were rough and almost impassable in winter. He kept four horses and usually drove to see his patients in a horse and buggy. If he anticipated a long rip he used two horses. If he found a patient very ill, he would stay in the home until he could see some improvement.

On one occasion, he was called to see a very ill patient in the Jones Spring area. He tied his two horses to a hitching post in front of the home. He remained quite a while with the patient and the horses broke loose from the post and returned home. Mrs. Ward heard them at the driveway gate. The doctor called later to check on the horses and to say that a member of the family would be bringing him home. .

In 1906 he built a home just north of the Hedgesville High School and on the side of the house he built a separate entrance and a place to see his patients. If they did come to call, sometimes they would have to wait for hours to see the doctor if he was out making calls. His wife would then invite them to eat with the family if they were there at meal time.

He bought medicine in large bottles and dispensed it to patients. He and Dr. T. K. Oates worked together in treating many patients. After consulting with Dr. Oates, often Dr. Ward would accompany a patient by train to John Hopkins Hospital for further treatment.

During the Flu epidemic of 1918 he was on the road visiting patients day and night. There were people who were ill everywhere.

His first automobile was a Stanley Steamer. The test of a good car at that time was fording a stream such as the Johnsontown Run. It was not unusual for his car to stop right in the middle of it as the water would put out the boiler and there would be no steam to operate the engine. He would have to get out and light a torch to heat water again in order to pump steam into the motor to start it running again.

He was frequently paid for his services with horse feed, hay or corn, or vegetables for family consumption. He was always grateful to patients who paid him in cash. Records revealed that he treated many patients who could never pay for his services.

Kathleen Johnson:

"Here is an incident in the life of **Dr. Thomas Lewis Harris.** Dr. Harris, the father of Thomas Lewis Harris, came to Hedgesville as a young physician. He married a young lady who was a governess at the home of Mr. Shields Payne. They had three children, two sons and a daughter. While the children were very young, Dr. Harris died and left Mrs. Harris to rear the three children.

It wasn't easy. The boys had to work as soon as they were old enough and big enough. They chopped kindling and carried wood, ran errands and did anything like they could to make a dime.

One of the boys, Lewis, decided that he wanted to be a doctor like his father. He went to the Hedgesville Elementary School and the high school. During the time that he was in high school this incident occurred which had far reaching consequences. Hedgesville used to have one- night shows at the old Masonic Hall near the Town Spring. Someone would come in advance and put up posters advertising the show. The shows would cost 10 cents, maybe 20 cents, but usually in that range. All the children would read the signs and wanted to go.

The night of this particular show, Lewis and his brother were at the door of the Hall and wanted very badly to see the show but didn't have the 30 cents necessary. Charlie Grabill saw the boys plight and the earnest looks they had about trying to see the show. Charlie decided to give them the entrance money. Lewis told Charlie that he would be repaid; he did not know when, but he knew that it would be so.

Lewis graduated from the Hedgesville High School but wanted to go to the University but had no money. He was told that if he went to the Berkeley County Court it might be possible that they would help him. So he went to see the members of the County Court in Martinsburg and somehow they either encouraged him or put him in touch with people who could help him because he went off to Morgantown.

After securing a job there he enrolled at West Virginia University. When he graduated he had money in the bank and he decided to further his education by being a surgeon. He enrolled in the Jefferson Medical College in Philadelphia, Pa.

Back home in Hedgesville, Charlie Grabill had met with a serious accident. He was kicked in the head by a mule. The doctors locally did what they could but he needed delicate surgery. Someone in the family said that perhaps Lewis Harris could help. When he heard of the situation he told the family to bring Charlie to Philadelphia immediately. They got on a train and went to Philadelphia and Charlie was operated on by skilled surgeons. He recovered and was able to return home. The costs of all of his expenses while there were borne by Dr. Harris to compensate him for that show ticket purchased many years before.

Later in life Dr. Harris became a very skilled surgeon and practiced in the area for many years. He later relocated his practice to Parkersburg, WV where he became very successful.

In June 1962 he returned to Hedgesville and spoke at the Hedgesville High School Alumni Association. At that time he left a sum of money in the bank to award seed money of $50. for a worthy senior to continue his/her education. This was known as the Harris Award.

He died in 1972 in Parkersburg as a very well to do man who had married twice to wealthy women.

Dr. Daniel Reed Ross – He moved from New York to Little Georgetown probably in 1865 where he taught school. In 1868 he went to Columbus, Ohio to attend medical college. He returned to Martinsburg to practice medicine in 1874-1876 then moved to North Mountain Depot. In 1877 he moved his practice to the Town of Hedgesville and stayed there until his death in 1924. He was also a surgeon for the B & O Railroad Relief Society.

Dr. George S. Hanna - received his license to practice medicine in Hedgesville, West Virginia in 1881. A graduate of the University of Maryland he established a medical practice in the town. He graduated in 1858 before the Civil War and came to the area in the 1881. He married Susan Luginbihl (?) and established a family. Their daughter, Susan Marian Hanna married Boyd Faulkner Kilmer. Dr. Hanna's grandchildren included : Boydy Virginia Kilmer Schneider,

Edward Kilmer, Dudley Benard Kilmer and George William Kilmer, Sr.

Daisy May Morrow: **Doctors Remembered**

" I believe the earliest doctors were Dr. Mitchell, Dr. Lemen and Dr. Harris. Dr. Clay went from Hedgesville to become a government doctor. Dr. Butler practiced in his house and had a drug store. Others were Dr. Hanna, Dr. Ross, Dr. Sponseller, Dr. Ward, Dr. Fry, Dr. Shipper, Dr. Shirley, Dr. Waters, and Dr. Helms

ORGANIZATION OF VILLAGE LIFE (1908 - 1919)

From Charles Ross:

The organization of the village life was very simple in those days. There was a Mayor or somebody that was the chief political officer in the town; as I remember Billy Poisal for many years held that important job. He may have had the rank of Town Sergeant. When anything happened that required the observation of somebody from the law, Mr. Billy Poisal would take over, accompanied by a deputy or two, and a lot of small boys, and go investigate whatever needed investigation.

We had a Fire Department in those days. It consisted of a series of ladders and some buckets which were housed in a long, low building that looked like an elongated dog house which had been extended to be about 20 feet long; that building was located just south of where the combined harness shop and barber shop was located.

If a fire unfortunately broke out ... and this was extremely rare, the ladders and the buckets were broken out in great haste and taken to where the fire occurred. Everyone rushed to the fire to do what they could and formed a bucket brigade.

But the singular thing about the fire department was that underneath the ladder building was stored what was known as the "*town decker.*" That term requires a little clarification. During the snow season in the winter, it used to get cold and quite a little snow settled in the gap of the mountain. Sled riding was the favorite sport as it should be in any hilly country; the small fry would go down the hills on sleds. If they did not have sleds they would take a shock of wheat to where the snow had become crusted and slide at a break neck rate down the hillsides no matter what they might hit at the bottom.

The young bloods of the town who wanted to go sledding in style chipped in together and had built, probably by the undertaker, Charlie Brown, who did that sort of thing.... a sled known as a double decker. Now this sled didn't have two decks but it was constructed in two parts, not like a bob sled. It consisted of a very long ordinary sled with good runners shod with steel, with a tongue protruding in front which was joined to a very short sled with wood runners shod with steel with a steering bar; and I dare say that this particular sled, the town decker, or short for the town double decker was used quite heavily by the young men in the town. I suspect that it was six to eight feet long or more.

For amusements you pretty much took care of it yourself. Rather than playing with toys you played with the world around you. There were hikes, swimming in Back Creek, which was called Back Crick in those days, skating on that body of water when it was frozen .... Or even on the Potomac River in the Long Pool which was across the river from Cherry Run along the canal. You could skate around the neck of Maryland stretching all the way from McCoy's Ferry past Little Georgetown at the foot of the neck end up the other side as far as Dam No. 5. You could skate two or three hours in one direction if the ice was smooth enough and of course, if you skated three hours in that direction.

Speaking of vehicles, no roads existed as we know them today. The best road that you could get was a road that periodically was surfaced with crushed lime stone, a little bit smaller than crop rock and a little bit bigger than gravel and that would be spread from crushers stationed at intervals along the road. The stone crusher would be there and loads of rock would come in and be crushed and then spread along the highway. The stone crusher would crush stone from one end and there would be macadam would come out the other side.

Automobile traffic was exceptional, so exceptional, that when an auto would pass by the house, we went to the forward of the fence to see it go by. *No one owned an automobile in Hedgesville prior to about 1909 or 1910.* I guess when Anna Mitchell purchased a car it was regarded as a great wonder.

Travel was by most part horse drawn vehicles, buggies for the most part, and there was another kind of luxury vehicle known as a "stick wagon." It was a good deal like a buggy except that it was manufactured without a top; it was a fair weather vehicle. There was a vehicle called a "Surrey" which was a wagon, small wagon, built on a light weight running gear and it had two transverse seats, which would take four passengers. The top was of linen or some other cloth, depending on the quality of the vehicle and frequently it was trimmed with a fringe. At one time the Mt. Clifton Hotel had its own private surrey for the purpose of transporting people between the North Mountain Depot and the Hotel.

The Mt. Clifton Hotel was a landmark in the community and was used for more pretentious parties both summer & winter. Dances were held there and gatherings. I remember there was a State Convocation of Episcopal Priests and that must have been quite an interesting experience.

It was a favorite resort of people from Washington, Baltimore, and Cumberland, probably as far back as the 1890s. It was patronized by "summer boarders"; those were people would like to come to the mountains to escape the heat of the city.

I do remember seeing up on the lawn at Mt. Clifton, a vivid recollection of young men and young women playing croquet. The young men would have white duck trousers, white canvas shoes, and striped blazers and sailor straw hats with fancy bands on them. My recollection was that the girls had regular Gibson Girl get ups with black skirts reaching to the ground, well stuffed with petticoats. They wore a blouse known a a shirtwaist, long sleeves, and pompadours with large sailor hats.

Every once in a while a young blood in Hedgesville would save up his money and buy a fine Hess buggy and a nice Buckskin horse, and a very elegant buggy whip, new harness, sometimes tan and sometimes black which he would keep polished and the brass work would shine to the last degree. It was about as good as you could do when you went a courting.

I would like to pay tribute to a very interesting nice old black man who had what was known as the "Star Route" That was a contract route hauling mail from the railroad station at North Mountain Depot to the Post Office at Hedgesville, now this man's name was Jake Thomas. He was friendly, generous, and known to all. Besides having an important government position like that, he had a regular routine. He had an old Union Army overcoat with a red lining which he used in bitter weather. It was a sight to behold to see this old man driving his mule and a rather decrepit light wagon much in need of repairs and very creaky. When facing a bitter wind going up the school house hill with the cape of the Union Army overcoat floating out behind him, he was a striking figure.

From James S. Pitzer:

When I was 12 years old I moved to Hedgesville and the fellows named Frank Harrison and Lew Harrison, 'tended the Hedgesville street lamps. They had coal oil lights, posts on each corner, and he would fill them up with coal oil in the evening and light them; and the next morning he would he would come by and blow out the lights. That was done every morning and night.

Then a fellow by the name of William Gordon put in acetylene lights and they had them only in a few months until electric lights come through so we done away with them.

Electric lights came in about 1926 or so and it wasn't very long getting people to hook up. The fellow named Shade wired our stone house.

The Council had to deal with electricity in Hedgesville. They wanted to have the street lights put in free through the town for the rights to wire all the other houses. The Council met but deadlocked. They sat up until about two o'clock in the morning to decide the issue. Charlie Rickard and Frank Rickard were on the Council and they got up and moved to allow the street lights to be billed at a "reasonable rate" and walked out. And that is how electricity came to Hedgesville.

I was on the Council off and on for forty years. The way we kept up the streets was difficult. One time, Cecil Wood, was Mayor and we five Councilmen, ordered a car load of fine stone to come to North Mountain Depot. We took Cecil's truck and we went down there and loaded it and then spread stones on the streets. That is the way that we kept the streets up off and on for about twenty years.

Where Fiery's lived, (Harley Miller house) I think is where Millers lived. They run a wholesale place. On the corner was a store. Over on the other corner Bealls, they had a store. Kreglow had a store on one corner and Beall had a store on the other. Across the street right above the Hedges store, Frank Jacques had a store until they moved to Winchester. William Poisal's store was up

the street going North. Right across from the spring, Mr. Jim Slaughter ran a store and a shoe store. After 1910 Mr. Branham and George Newkirk ran a store where the Odd Fellows Hall is.
Up the street, on Church Street, Miss Phoebe Harrison did sewing and everything for clothes. I used to take my clothes up there and she would clean them and press them. We had a tin shop here in Hedgesville, close to the Slaughter's store and run by a man named Stewart Harrison.

From Frances Brown Pearrell:

The shoemaker was John Guinn; he had his shoemaker shop down there near the Spring. He lived up on what we called Potato Hill, but he came down there every day, and he had a wooden leg. He was crippled. I don't know how he lost it but he had a wooden leg. He had a very small shop.

One Halloween the boys got a cow somehow and got it in his building and they just couldn't turn that cow around - had to back her out so you know the cow would leave. It took them quite a while to get that done.

The same Halloween, they put a buggy on

top of a stable roof at Dr. Fry's house. How they ever got it up there, I don't know.

We had two dressmakers - Miss Annie Kreglow and Miss Bert Small and the Bodine girls- Ida and Flora but later they left to work in Martinsburg

The Kreglows lived in the place that was Dr. Butler's drug store. Then next to him was Dr. Grabill's dentist office; and it was just stacked with newspapers from the year one. Then the next was a little building that Miss Annie Kreglow used to have a millinery shop and then in the other end of the house she and her mother lived. Of course, right across the alley was the tailor shop.

When my father, C. M. Brown, had the Post Office, there was a man here called Hawley Robinson and he carried the mail to and from North Mountain with his mail pouch on his back. Then a black man, Jake Thomas, did it when Bern Kilmer was here. Jake was so irritated that he would come down there every morning to the Post Office and it would not be open. He carried the mail to and from North Mountain Depot with a pack on his back.

When my father was post master, there was a man at Jones Spring that had a right big store. It was Charlie James and he used to send his money to the bank and it was always a Registered Letter. Well the mail was put on a pole, I don't know whether you would call it a crane or not, and then they come along on the mail train and jerk it off into the car. Well, this time there was an incident that I never forgot. I had handled the registered mail that evening. Somehow the registered letter with the money in it was lost! Well, Daddy was just worried to death of course. He came out to school and had me tell him what I did about locking up the pouch and all. This went on for a long, long time and after searching, it was finally declared a loss. One day somebody was coming along the railroad tracks and they looked down to discover that the pouch had fallen and was covered partially in mud. They delivered it to the post office and all the money was in it and safe.

Daisy May Morrow recalls Hedgesville :

"When I was a child I spent six months near Hedgesville with a cousin, Mrs. Edith Eichelberger. We often came to Hedgesville to the stores and to visit friends. Once we visited the Payne family at the new Mt. Clifton Hotel. We attended the new Presbyterian Church and the "Old Brick" Methodist Church. I liked to see the man lighting the street lights on poles. He carried a short ladder with him to get up on the poles.

I enjoyed going into the stores. The penny candies were a great, and the stores smelled so of a mixture of fish, tobacco, and a lot of other things that made each store have an odor all of its own.

Personality Notables :

John Ellis & Morgan Shaffer by Charlie Ross

John Ellis was a very agreeable, very singular man, very agreeable and he had a great liking for boys welfare. I have sat in his establishment watching him repair harness and skillfully cut out leather and rapidly stitch it .... And so forth but I think his greatest claim to fame was that he cut hair for 15 cents on Saturday nights. The elder boys, who were old enough to get shaved before they went out on their Saturday night date, would come in to get their shave in an old wooden barber chair which was completely operated by hand. The chair was equipped with a razor strap and John had razors, hones, etc. but his hot water apparatus was very singular. It consisted of a tea kettle that sat on a pot bellied stove – that was the hot water for shaving. He had an enamel wash basin which served the further purposes of shaving.

Then there was another citizen who was unique and well liked, he was the late Morgan Shaffer. Morgan's father had been a wagon maker in the days when wagons were not bought from catalogs or farm implement dealers but you went to Mr. Shaffer and told him what kind of wagon you wanted and the purpose you wanted it used for; for instance there were wagons for use on the farm, there were wagons for hauling things on the road from the farm to the railroad station for shipment by freight; and then there was a type of wagon which was used to haul bark from the Back Creek Valley down to North Mountain Depot for shipment to the tanneries. The bark wagon was a peculiar type of wagon, they resembled the Conestoga wagon, the prairie schooner. They had a kind of dip and curve to the top line and the front of the wagon dipped out, and the back of the wagon dipped out, and they were reinforced, and if somebody had some stanchions and canvas to cover it they would have looked just like the prairie schooners that you read about. These wagons creaked up and down the road there, loaded down, toward North Mountain Depot, past Dr. Ross house. There was a bucket of tar known of course as the "Tar Bucket" which is the days before Standard Oil Co, was to lubricate bearings on which the wheels operated. They were drawn by four horses, teams of horses in tandem, the two leaders in front, and the two wheel horses attached by single trees to the rear. The wagon pull was between them and the near horse was the one on the left side, and the off horse was the one on the right side. So the near wheeler, beside having to pull his share of the load, had to carry the driver on his back, who generally drove with one reign, by voice commands to the leaders to go right to left, or from left to right, which were known as "Gee" for left and "Haw" for right. They negotiated the trip from back in the mountains down to North Mountain Depot all through the seasons.

William M. Shaffer by Mary Unger Hite .....

William M. Shaffer and Mary Virginia Swingle were married April 12, 1849. They came to Hedgesville as a bride and groom and found rooms in the large brick house that was torn down to make way for the brick post office on Main Street.

He was my grandfather and he often told us that there were only two houses and the Episcopal Church here at that time. He built the long house between Ludwig's and James Poisal.

My father, Jacob Unger, came from Little Georgetown and married Annabell Shaffer. He bought and opened a General Store in the house on Mary Street where Ruppenthal's now live. Later he sold the store to Mr. William "Uncle Billy" Poisal. He then built and opened a flour and feed mill at the corner next to the Episcopal Church. The building known as the spray plant was destroyed by fire in 1962, catching the Mt. Zion Episcopal Church roof on fire and nearly burning it down also.

[Mary Kate Eckerd was in her majorette outfit and walking up the hill to the high school when she spotted the smoke coming out of the roof of the church. She rushed to the building and met Jimmy Poisal at the front door where they hurriedly entered. The fire was located toward the north end and they decided they should try to save the pulpit which was the heaviest item in the structure! With providential strength they were able to get it lose from its moorings and with a lift, slide, push arrangement they got it to the back of the building toward the vestibule. They then turned their attention to saving what they could inside the building. Ancient prayer books and hymnals were pitched through the window glass on the east side of the building and out onto the grass. Other communion items, bibles, and important documents were carried outside. By this time help had arrived and other people rushed to move things out of the building. The roof came crashing through the ceiling and nothing more could be done to the inside. ...from a statement ... by Mary Kate Moore]

Maude Mason Remembers:

I was one of three children of Clarence Thomas & Mamie V. Mason, who served as lifetime custodians at Hedgesville High School. Both the one torn down in 1926 and the new one built the following year. Mrs. Marshall (Naomi Blakes) was born in Hedgesville in 1894. Her mother died when she was six weeks old so she was raised by her grandmother, Mrs. Charles Jones. She went to Locust Knob school.

Maurie (Marie) Mason moved to Hedgesville from Front Royal, VA with a family named Bushotter. [*He was George Bushotter, a Sioux Indian, who had recruited blacks and Indians to settle in the area after he graduated from Hampton School in Hampton, VA]* Marie worked as a house maid bringing with her a small son, William. As a boy William worked for various farmers, and when he grew up he married the step daughter of Jake Thomas, purchased a small orchard from which he sold apples to a concern in Havre-de-Grace, Maryland. He later opened a watch repair shop in his home. From these two trades he was able to raise a family of six sons, and one daughter.

Two children still living are Charles Jr, Mason of Hagerstown, and Dora Lee, who lives in a home near the entrance to her father's orchard. Others living on what was once the Will Mason Orchard property are Clarence Mason, Charles Mason, Juanita Williams, and some grandchildren.

Thomas Mason bought some of the lumber from Mr. Cecil Woods when the Mt. Clifton Hotel was torn down, and built the Mason home which is still occupied by his son Clarence Mason and family, and the sister Maude. They still have a bath tub and wash bowl with marble top and slab at the back which once belonged in Mt. Clifton. They also have a W. E. Mason Jewelry Case.

Other residents we remember are William Pulpus who hauled passengers to and from North Mountain Depot by horse and carriage and raised six children from just this income. Henry Holly, a carpenter's helper and his wife Anna Holly who was a licensed mid-wife, raised eight children. Eliza Johns, married Frank Johns, a lifetime worker in Bessemer Quarry. She was well known for her cooking ability, and cooked for the contractors who built the Hedgesville High School in the 1920s. George Washington Thompson was

the long time barber in Hedgesville and cut the hair of several generations of people in his little shop.
Burrell Snyder and his wife Clara, gave music lessons to community children. Mr. Snyder was very versatile and went into many ventures, some of which include a general store, a music shop; he obtained a printing press from which he published the town's newspaper THE BERKELEY ENTERPRISE. He also had a donut shop, and a farm where he experimented with chickens and cattle breeding. George Phoenix, owned a small Model T Ford, and operated the first taxi cab service in Hedgesville.

The Misses Alice & Fannie Ronk operated the switch board from their dining room, taking care of all the telephone calls going in and out of the Hedgesville exchange until the dial system was installed. The dial system building was located on Mary Street and the Ronk sisters checked in at the dial house until their retirement.

We credit these people with having "down to earth" talents in that they were able to maintain a home, and raise a family with very little income, and very little formal education, but very fortunate in having common sense."

Vallie Virginia Henshaw – by Katherine Butler Heiskell

My great Aunt, Vallie Virginia Henshaw, a resident of Hedgesville and prominent among educators of Berkeley County, began her teaching in the rural schools of the county. She formed the first Chapter of the Daughters of American Revolution (DAR) to be organized in West Virginia. It was formed on April 8, 1899 and is known as the Capt. William Henshaw Chapter, NSDAR. She was the first Regent and during her regency four other chapters were formed.

She married Francis O. Berry who lived in Texas and lived there for several years; failing in health, she returned to West Virginia for several years. She died June 4, 1927 and is buried in the Hedgesville Cemetery where a state NSDAR brass plaque has been erected in her memory.

Undertakers and stuff ....

By J. S. Pitzer:

We had two undertakers in the town. Mr. Jacques was the undertaker – that's on the corner of the store ... and Mr. Charlie Brown had his undertaking shop right below his house in a little building. There were some undertakers before Jacques & Brown – his name was Furon and I understand that he taught these men undertaking.

[The *process of undertaking was quite different in those times. There were no "funeral homes" where the deceased was on view and people came to call. Funerals were conducted in the home or church and many times the process of embalming was conducted right there in the home also. The shops that were spoken of just existed to store equipment and materials. The type of coffin might be what was available in size but many cases the casket was made by the undertaker for that person.]*

Hedgesville did not have any large church cemetery but there was a cemetery located beside the Mt. Zion Episcopal Church.
An association was organized Dec. 17, 1881 to organize & maintain a public cemetery. The following individuals served as members: John W. Hedges, E. G. Manor, George Kreglow, W. H. Kilmer, M.S. Butts,

Decatur Hedges and J. H. Alexander. These men had a vision that a cemetery was needed for the good of the community. The incorporation was recorded in Corporate Record Book 1, Page 41 in the Berkley County Court House.]

By Frances Brown Pearrell .....

My father, Charles Brown, had his funeral department and funeral home here next to this house here at the corner; we always called the Wolfe's house because Charlie Wolfe owned it then. We lived there until he bought up on Mary Street and when Dad bought he got the Post Office and we probably moved up in 1897 or 98. The shop was built and the post office was in the back. He did other work beside that. They were always calling them undertaker-cabinet maker because he did a lot of repairing furniture and making new furniture.

The funeral directors made their own coffins. They were narrow at the bottom and wider at the top according to the fashion of the time. They were not rectangular like they are now. They way they would get them to bend at the corners; they sawed at intervals, to make them bend. Of course, they had nothing but boards and they covered them and padded them on the inside, and then sometimes they would put some kind of covering on the outside... or if they had time, they would stain them.

Then there was always a rough box that went into the grave. At that time I don't think there were any vaults, once in a while they might have muslin to line the grave but they never had any vault.

The cost was many times what the person could pay but I recall that my father used to have a $75. Funeral and he thought that was tops.

Later on they would buy their caskets from the city; but they weren't always lined and so they had to be lined. They had their own material and they would line them by using excelsior and padded them with cotton or something softer and they always made a little pillow for in the box.

Mr. Jacques and my Dad had their own hearses. Of course the driver would sit out in front – there was no covering over them-there was a seat out in front. There was a glassed in part of the hearse where the body was placed in the casket. They were painted all black with brass coach lights toward the front.

R. A. Jacques....

Mr. Jacques was a highly skilled cabinet maker which meant that he could build things from houses to furniture. His family came from one of the first families to settle in Berkeley County via Clear Spring, MD. He erected a home and had a cabinet shop. He later went into the undertaking business as a logical extension of his carpentry business. His undertaking shop was on the square where he kept his equipment and materials. His house was destroyed by fire and another structure built by James Conklyn in 1935

THE MOUNT CLIFTON HOTEL
BY CARL HOWARD

It was quite a sight. As visitors carriages left the train station and ascended a hill just beyond Hedgesville's Main Street, the grand three story hotel suddenly came into view.

The Town of Hedgesville was a tourist destination for city folk wanting to get away from the summer heat in places like Washington, DC, Baltimore, and even Philadelphia. They came by train, the Baltimore & Ohio line. Horse-drawn carriages met them at the North Mountain Station Depot, where rail tracks now intersect Route 901 on the eastern edge of town.

The carriages bustled them the mile's distance into the village and briefly onto what was then known as Warm Springs Road (now heavily traveled Route 9 west), as it swung up the lower slopes of High Knob, the highest of the North Mountain overlooking Hedgesville.

Hotel guest, weary of the cities' busy 1890's

social whirl of winter, had found a peaceful summer nook far enough away to escape the heat & grime of urban life. This was, as advertised, " a first class place for those who are seeking health & rest."

Often it was moms and children who came and stayed at length
("special terms for families and those engaging board for prolonged periods"), some for an entire summer. Hedgesville's resort hotel gave them a place to "sit and rock", talk, take side trips , and play games on the lawn. The women sewed and did "fancy work", and meeting new friends. They brought along nursemaids for the small ones. Husbands would come from the cities on weekends. The trip from Washington took just two hours and from Baltimore, it was perhaps three hours.

So, people swarmed in. Sometimes as many as 80 to 90 were accommodated, at one time in the 22 room addition that an enterprising couple, Mr. & Mrs. Tripp Payne, built onto their home in 1893. Room and board was $5 weekly for adults and half price for children. Overflow crowds were housed at the Summit House across the street--- a large residence still standing across Main

Street from the Hedgesville Presbyterian Church --- as well as other homes in the village. Topnotch meals for all were supplied in the dining room of the hotel.

Mrs. Nannie Payne herself supervised the cooking, with hired help from the town. According to the advertising, "Cuisine and service unexcelled. Table supplied with fresh, pure, and wholesome food. Fruits, such as peaches, apples, pears, and plums (if the season affords) furnished in great quantities."

A well remembered bellhop, Jimmie Thompson, cut wood and carried it to the guest's rooms --- if they stayed on into cooler weather.

But the hotel management mainly was a family endeavor. Will Payne, son of the proprietors, busied himself in entertaining guests. He would take them on trips around the countryside, using a four-horse wagon. The Hotel advertised that "surrounding country abounds in pleasing road scenery and good roads, making riding and driving a delight. Plenty of game abounds in the mountains and surrounding country. There is splendid bass fishing in Back Creek, one mile and the Potomac River, two miles distant." Some say that Potato Hill Street on the west side of Hedgesville got its name from Will as he drove tourists past a large field where potatoes grew. Will was heading up the hill to show visitors an early settlement called "Kate's Hollow" on a trail that led out of town toward the community of Allensville.

The hotel guests also enjoyed "city ways" at their country inn. Saturday night dances were held in a large first-floor ballroom that featured handsomely polished wood floors. In the daytime, light entering through large, long windows gleamed on the dark wooden surfaces. At night, a large gas-light chandelier cast prism reflections across the room.

Memories included the names of Marshall Mason, Tom Mason, and Richard Bennett as musicians whose band played for "tripping the light fantastic."

Out- of- towners weren't the only ones who enjoyed the Mt. Clifton Hotel Ballroom. A committee of townspeople also arranged dances by invitation, though events at the hotel were so greatly admired that folks often "crashed" the party. The Hotel, of course, was fashionable as well for local society, and romances blossomed from events in the ballroom and dining room. Will Payne married Gertrude Price, daughter of the local Methodist Minister, at high noon on October 17, 1900 and the church wedding was followed by sumptuous luncheon at the hotel.

Summer delights at Mt. Clifton also featured social hours on the three story hotel's large front and west side porches. The view of the valley below was fantastic --- ranging from the blue mountains to Frederick County, Maryland, to the gap that led to Harpers Ferry. A "widow's walk" atop the building offered the very best view. And a second floor wooden bridge on the back of the structure led to a nearby grove of trees.

Young men in white duck trousers, white canvas shoes, striped blazers and straw hats played croquet on the hotel's lawn. Their ladies were Gibson girl fashion with long skirts stuffed with petticoats, their hair in pompadour style and topped with large sailor hats. Stylishly dressed players enjoyed a clay tennis court at the side of the hotel, where small shards of clay are still found on a level area of the slope.

Adventurous hotel guests and local folks climbed up the mountain to the point called "High Knob" Apparently, an observation tower site at the very top it was used by troops on one side or other during the Civil War, and for tourists it now afforded an even more pleasing view of the valley below.

The Paynes were successful entrepreneurs, and did well with the summer boarder business. When one of Hedgesville's most memorable fires destroyed the impressive Victorian structure in 1902, they promptly rebuilt Mt. Clifton Hotel. It now had 36 rooms, featuring massive timbers and rafters. The new hotel was bigger and better than ever!

But times were changing. Hotel patronage began to fade. In 1904, the Paynes sold the hotel to R. B. and Sarah Kilmer. The Kilmers at first attempted to rent out apartments, although that effort was met with limited acceptance. The building was constructed for summer use, and it was impossible to heat adequately when winter came.

So the Kilmers returned to the summer

resort trade, advertising in this way:

Season of 1907 ... A popular home Resort in the Heart of the Mountains.... Renovated and remodeled- R. B. Kilmer, Prop. A First Class Place for those who are seeking health and rest... Your correspondence solicited. Terms $6 to $10 per week.

Indeed, the hotel had been thoroughly renovated, with new furniture in its large, cheerful and beautifully appointed rooms. It featured pure mountain water from its own artesian well.

The hotel now boasted of private baths, sun parlors, and of course, the "porches" and a "beautiful grove", and the tennis courts on the grounds.

The automobile was changing vacation preferences, and the hotel's glory days were numbered. Guest reservations declined year by year. Eventually the Mt. Clifton more resembled a rooming/boarding house than a hotel. Then, although the exact date is not known, Mt. Clifton Hotel closed its doors.

In 1925-1926 the Mt. Clifton Hotel found a new purpose and for one was totally unique. The local school built of brick in the 1880's had become unstable and dangerous. In high winds the upper floor shook furiously and classes could not be held there.
It was condemned. There was a fervid campaign to find a way to replace the building, even going so far as to try public subscription and out- right pleas for money. The local governmental district did not have any industry for taxation purposes until a local physician came up with the idea that the
B & O railroad crossed through the taxation area and was a business and therefore it should be taxed. It took a wrangling through the courts, but finally the Railroad did pay the tax and enough money was obtained to built a new school.

Where would the children go to school while the new one was built? Simple. They just rented the Hotel property and fitted it out so classes could be held there. So for that one year 1925-26, all of the grades of the school from grade one through grade twelve attended that building.

Then in 1927, a change in the Warm Springs

Road (now Route 9) caused a major indignity to the hotel site: The road from Martinsburg formerly climbed up a fairly steep slope and ran right in front of the hotel. Growing use of the auto had created an issue; the Model T couldn't always make it up that steep grade. So a notch was cut in the hill and, Route 9 was moved down to its present location some distance before it passes in front of the Hedgesville Presbyterian Church and it becomes the town's Main Street.

In 1920, a local physician and land speculator, Dr. T. K. Oates, purchased the hotel building for $2,175 after the property had become embroiled in a court suit. Dr. Oates reportedly proposed making a hospital or sanitarium of the building, but that plan failed to materialize. He later founded a hospital in Martinsburg that later became City Hospital

At any rate, in 1930, the building and grounds were sold to Cecil W. Wood, who by that time owned property on both sides of the hotel. In the economic situation of the times, Mr. Wood saw no commercial value to the building, so he salvaged it for materials. The barn-sized girders and beams were especially attractive and found eager buyers. The lumber was repurposed to build several other homes. The window frames were removed and can still be seen in several homes around Hedgesville town. Scrap lumber went into apple boxes for Mr. Wood's orchards.

Thus ends the story of the little Hedgesville's Victorian era glory as a summer resort, Mt. Clifton Hotel, in its hey-day, was a special place on the end of the North Mountain outcropping where it perched above the Shenandoah Valley.

Mt. Clifton Hotel, R. Bernard Kilmer, Prop., Hedgesville, W. Va.

GLEANINGS FROM THE TOWN MINUTE BOOK 1905-1947

1905 – Still haven't paved streets – trying to rent stone crusher from the County Court at 5 cents a perch. [Apparently in April of that year it was done]

April, 1906 – E. P. Beall was notified to repair his scales to weigh wagons coming into town or remove within ten days.

May, 1906 - … clear all wagons, parts, lumber, trash from vacant lot between Masonic and Odd Fellows Hall.

May, 1907 – The full oath of office was officially listed in the minute book.

June, 1907 – Council gave Mr. Frank Rickard permission to place town lamp at the Town Spring at his expense for one year.

September, 1907 – J. T. Unger makes application to build a grist mill, corner of his lot – north of Episcopal Church – 22 x 54

July, 1908 – bridges [wooden planks across drainage ditches] at John Street choked up at the foot of the hill after a bad rain. Also bridge on Church Street needs attention.

March, 1909 – Mr. John A. Rickard, presented a 2,000 candle power gasoline arc light – not nearer than 20 feet from ground. Council will maintain and buy gasoline – to be lighted 22 nights monthly – M. S. Butler & Locke Beall were to light the lights.

Suggestion of the Mayor June 6, 1910 - A statement:

" As we are about to enter the discharge of the duties conferred upon us by the voters of the village, I have thought it best to make some suggestions as we should be governed in the administration of the affairs of the corporation.

I would suggest first with reference to the improvement of the streets, that due regard should be had for each and every section of the town giving its fair and proper share, so that all the citizens may feel that our citizens are justified to continue the fair proportion of taxes to meet the indebtedness thus incurred .

Secondly, with reference to the lighting of

the lamps, I would recommend that some arrangement be made for lighting the lamps not spasmodically, but, regularly for a stated number of nights each month. I believe that if this is done, the tax payers will be willing to pay their share of the taxes necessary to carry on...

Thirdly, the condition of the Town Spring and the uses made of it by evil persons .... It is a shame and reproach to any community and demands immediate attention.

Fourth, the alleys of the town .... Many of them are in bad condition from a sanitary point of view and call for some attention.

Fifth, while it may be early to take up the matter of assessment and taxation, we must not lose sight of so important a matter, and while the interest of the taxpayer should be carefully guarded at the same time, it is very important the levy should be sufficient to meet the demands made upon it to properly carry on the affairs of the corporation.

Last, it is the matter of maintaining law and order in the village and to suppress some of the conditions of things, I earnest request and shall confidently respect your cordial and individual support.

In conclusion, I beg to assure you that you shall at all times have my earnest support in everything that pertains to the betterment of the municipal government of the town.

Signed: George F. Kreglow – Mayor May 6, 1910

August, 1910 – Town budget levy was $310. First mention of automobiles speed to be 6 miles per hour – ordinance prepared by E. N. Rickard. Robert Hull is to light the lights in the village.

November 1910 – Vacant lot in front of the Episcopal Church transferred from ownership of A. H. Alexander to the Church.

Feb. 6, 1911 – Town spring house building sold to A. H. Myers for $3.00 and told to remove it as soon as possible.

June 20, 1911 – Council put galvanized roof on the building over the spring. The rafters were too light for slate, and they also repaired the wall. Sergeant William Poisal made an arrest and conveyed a prisoner to the County jail. Received $2.00 in fee.

September 1911 - Crossing 12″ tile - reinforced with wire and cement to replace some of the foot bridge – on Mary Street

May, 1912 - Mayor John A. Rickard to purchase a book to be known as Mayor's docket and to recall all town business in it. The big problem was throwing old tin cans and garbage in the streets. It now costs $75 to light the town streets.

July, 1912- E. H. Bender, representing C & P Telephone Co, made an application for a franchise to erect, and operate.

August, 1912 - Contract made with W.E. Gordon of Martinsburg for the Hedgesville Light & Heat Company permit to establish, erect, and operate an acetylene light and heat plant for 20 years for a payment of $65 per year. He agreed to furnish street lights – one of 50 candle power and 7 of 35 candle power.

October, 1912 - To light the street lights: October 1 to March 31st the lights be on from 5:30 to 1:00 a.m. for 15 hours; From April 1 until Sept 30th from 8:00 to 11:00. They were to be on for a total of 264 nights a year.

September 3, 1912 – A contract with C & P Telephone – they could assign, construct, maintain poles, ditches and cables ... on and along the right of way for a period of 50 years.

April, 1913 – Capon Power Co – Application to erect, poles, string wires through town. Tabled – but franchise granted in May.

August, 1913 – Reference was made to the scales to weigh wagons coming into town for taxes on Mary & Main Streets. They are out of order.

Feb., 1914 – Ordered notice in Martinsburg newspaper for 400 perch of limestone to repair streets for "as far as it would go."

April, 1914 – Health Officer received $5 for Council. The Sergeant to serve notice on Dr. Shipper, F. L. Beall, to repair and replace their sidewalks.

May, 1914 – Council voted to connect to electric lights and to have them burn all night for ten streets at $1.20 per year.

July, 1915 - $20 for electric bill for the town.

May, 1916 – June 6th set for "Clean Up Day". Something happened – the record book gets sparse – little seems to be happening then F. B. Beall is made Mayor pro-tem until J. A. Rickard returns or resigns.

March 6, 1917 – T.L. Beall, Mayor, called the meeting to order.

May 1, 1917 – Two copies of the charter of Hedgesville to be written off by Miss Agness Voegell. Governor John Cornwell sent a letter requesting the names of every unemployed man in the community. [it was World War I]

Nov., 1917 – J. C. Ellis sent by council to see Prosecuting Attorney in reference to running horses loose in the streets.

July 1919- Town Sergeant, W. W. Faulkwell is bonded.

July, 1920 – Street Superintendent, E. E. Claybaugh ordered to set watering trough as he thinks best. Citizens pitched in with $47 to oil the streets to cut down the dust.

September 30, 1920 – Electric lights ordered placed on Potato Hill and Window Street (ne Church St) . Tile was to be placed in front of Masonic Hall.

December, 1920 – Permit Granted Orchard Supply Co (Landis & Wood) to put building on the Unger Mill foundation. To manufacture and sell orchard supplies, including operation of a steam engine. G. W. Poisal installed gas tank in front of his house.

January, 1921 - Quay Keesecker put gas tank in front of his shop.

May, 1921- hay scales placed in front of Dr. J. H. Shipper's house – purchased from Mr. McClure for $50. Price fixed at 10 cents per draft- G. W. Poisal weigh master at 50% commission on scales. Bud Wasson paid $5.25 for work on streets.

May 11, 1921 – Resolution of Mayor Cecil Wood: Charges of fraud not substantial. Charges by J. M. Vermilyea, Dr. Grabill, A. C. Stewart...for irregularities of the commissioners...

May 16, 1921 – Noise of muffler cut outs

causing concern of citizens – fireworks also – lights of the town spring and a complaint that Mr. George Olinger be replaced.

June, 1922 – Notify Thomas Holmes that his barking dog has become a nuisance. Mr. W. Avey relative 10 wagons being packed at Masonic Hall. All our town meat vendors charged $12 per year.

October 1922 – Mayor executed a deed conveying to the County Court, a 40 foot right of way from the Eastern Limit of corporation to the Masonic Hall to build a slate road.

May, 1923 – J.D. Stuckey builds a concrete sidewalk. C. W. Keesecker build a front porch and a concrete pavement.

August, 1923 –State Road not granted permission to run drain water down alley by Dr. Fry's stable. Ladder house moved to Odd Fellows Hall.

December, 1923- Notify state Road – remove stump and fill up hole in front of the Presbyterian Church.

July, 1924 - Arrests in the town:
Lee Albright, speeding $2.50, E. J. Everhart $3.50, Harry Everhart $5.50, and G. W. Poisal $3.00.

July 1924 - Mr. Vermilyea ordered to fill in pavement as well as Mrs. Bear and C. J. Newkirk - all four foot concrete within 30 days. G. W. Poisal permit to erect 25 x 34 frame building on Miller lot.

July, 1924 - Complete motor vehicle laws were enacted via the State of West Virginia.

August, 1925 - 13 people arrested for failure to note motor vehicle laws - Leon Edwards, Ralph Lewis, J. W. Kearns, & C. W. Spiker.

February, 1925 - Residents must have building permits before they begin work. Detailed ordinance was filed.

August ,1925 - County Court obtained right of way and its relationship to the water trough at the town spring was listed. The degrees and feet were listed.

Mrs. C. M. Brown, C. W. Wood put down sidewalk. J.N. Miller put up front porch.

August, 1925 - Street Supervisor, C. H. Rickard , reported there is an urgent need of more stone and tar for street surfacing.

August, 1925 – ordered hog pen and chicken yard of C. J. Grabill be declared a public nuisance and removed.

December, 1925 - Permit - Presbyterian Chapel build wall and 4 foot sidewalk, C.W. Wood - wall in front of his property ... L. W. Johnson build smoke & wash house.

December, 1925 - Committee of citizens concerned about fire hazards and water supply for fire protection.

January, 1926 – J.W. Poisal was given permit to install gasoline tank and pump in front of his store on Main Street.

May, 1926 – Another "Whereas Almighty God in his Wisdom" has summoned .... A resolution was made by the council for Wm. L. Ellis at his passing.

January, 1927 - Scarlet Fever Epidemic has hit the town. Many are sick. Mayor consulted with Health Department to asses if there is anything being done to check the epidemic.

June, 1927 – Hedgesville enacted Prohibition ordinances consistent with the state ones.

June 1927 – W. H. Lemen and L. W. Johnson acted as a committee to decide location of lights and telephone poles between the school house and R. K. Pearell's. Paving of street from Main Street to the School house was done with the County Court paying for it.

July, 1927 – L. J. Landis builds 7 foot porch in front of house.

December, 1927 The wall at Johnson's property and the street done by the town for $198 Bill Chambers, Harvey Pearell, J. H. Morgan, G. W. Poisal, E. H. Mussetter did the work.

August , 1928 – By-laws of the City of Martinsburg, were adopted and adapted to the Town of Hedgesville.

October , 1928 – J. W. Poisal be appointed to collect the taxes of the corporation.

December, 1928 - Council decided to put slate on streets at crossing of Newkirks, Stuckeys, and Ronks.

April, 1929 - Dr. Shirley was granted a permit to build a two story brick veneered house with fire proof roof on the "Shaffer lot" joining Lester Landis - cost $6,000 with George Kitchen as contractor.

June 4, 1929 - Charles Shipper was arrested June 3rd for disorderly conduct and was fined $6.50 which he refused to pay. Mayor A. H. Mitchell sentenced him to the County jail for 30 days for contempt of court.

September, 1929 - Moved & seconded that Council set a standard of 25 cents per hour for labor for the corporation. Moved & seconded that Kathleen Johnson make out the tax bills for the present year.

Feb., 1930 - G. W. Poisal was granted a permit to build a " bungalow"

August, 1930 - Post Office was granted permit to put up porch to receive mail. Moved & seconded notify Coe Riner if he can't get water from the town spring without stirring up the water, he will be compelled to cease from using it.

Dec,1939 - Mr. J. C. Ellis makes permit to install a gas tank at his house.

April, 1931 - James Pitzer granted a permit to improve his property by building a wall at St. Marks Church.

July, 1931 - Town Sergeant - J. D. McCarty to receive a salary of $50 for the year

Nov.,1931 - Hugh DeHaven was notified he will be required to pay a license to the town of $50 a year in advance for permission to operate a pool hall, but not on Sunday.

Jan, 1932 - Council returned a vote of thanks to the Mayor J. M. Vermilyea for his very able and efficient manner of conducting his affairs of his office as Mayor of the municipality. The street supervisor, C. H. Rickard, was ordered to have a good cap built over the town spring that will exclude dirt and filth from it. The material shall be well seasoned, tongue and grooved lumber with a door at the top, large enough to admit a fair sized bucket.

August, 1932 - The sergeant was ordered to

notify C. W. Kitchen to put his dog somewhere so that the howling and the barking at night will not hinder his neighbors from their sleep and rest.

August, 1933 – Ed Ambrose is to make a STOP sign to place at the entrance of the High School.

Dec, 1933 – Elmer Lucas, Marvin Ellis, & M.A. Robbins appointed on the committee for the layout of work for Mr. Tabler, the foreman of the R.T. C. workers [National Industry Recovery Act workers for public works]

December, 1933 – Mrs. Brown deeds a strip of land to the town for the continuation of an alley leading through to St. Johns Road [now Potato Hill]

April, 1934 – James S. Pitzer was elected Mayor for the unfinished term of G. W. Poisal, who died. In resolution stating "Our town has lost of its best citizens, a faithful Mayor, and member of this Council."

August 8, 1934 – Tile leading across street by the Old Brick Church ordered covered with slate.

January, 1935 – Council moved from the Poisal room into the room of R. A. Jacques at $10 per year for a meeting place.

March, 1935 – Council agreed to get two new fire ladders and six canvas buckets; ladder house to be painted white & green. James Conklin was granted a permit to build a one story house 30x32 ½ on a lot bought by Mrs. G. Williams.

April, 1936 – Dr. Shipper was granted a permit to build a bay window in house occupied by R. A. Jacques providing it was kept back off the present pavement line.

April, 1937 – Council then decided to sponsor a WPA project for work in the Hedgesville Cemetery.

1938 – A permit was issued to James Poisal to place a stand on the side of his store roof parallel to the State Road.

March, 1939 – A permit was issued to the Trustees of the Episcopal Church to build a concrete walk on their church property.

June, 1938 – First complete list of ordinances

mentioned.
Example: Section 14: "that if any person wantly molest or insult any person whatsoever, when going to or returning from religious meeting and within 100 yards of holding the same; or if anyone should be found idly loitering at or near the door of any church, or religious meeting and when requested to do so, shall be quietly and peaceably depart from thence, or if any person shall behave rudely, disorderly, or insulting in any church, meeting house, or other place of public worship, every person upon conviction shall pay a fine of $10, not exceeding, $200.

Aug., 1939 – A briar scythe was ordered purchased at $3.06; Ted Laign paid $2.00 for labor in using it to cut down weeds.

Nov., 1939 – Motion made and passed that runway on scales be widened to permit both wheels of dual trucks on run on same.

May, 1940 – A permit was granted Jacob Poisal to built bay window in warehouse.

March, 1941 – A permit was granted to J. S. Pitzer to build an addition to his property known as the Old Stone House.

Aug, 1944- Motion was made and seconded for Mr. Landis to take out the scales if they are worth repairing. Also for Mr. Landis to store them until they can be put in a new location.

September, 1944 – James. W. Poisal was granted a permit to build a lunch room on his lot, also to drain the basement of same building into the drain in the alley.

June, 1947 – Motion approved to secure sufficient labor to clean the Town Spring, repair, concrete in and around the spring, paint building, and cut grass around the spring. '

September, 1947 – It was unanimously approved that 20 or more letters be sent out to persons in the vicinity of Hedgesville asking their cooperation to establish a volunteer fire company for Hedgesville & the surrounding areas.

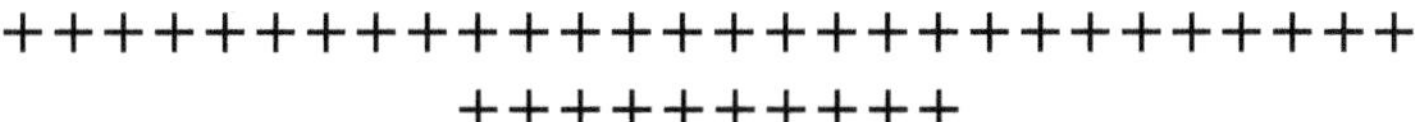

And so we close this historical effort just as Hedgesville is poised to accomplish some of its most significant events for its citizenry. Through cooperative efforts with community and county efforts, it did establish a Fire Department, it did create a Public Service District that brought public water and later public sewage systems, and it did help continue the designation of a new high school as Hedgesville High School. In 1976 in competition with towns its size throughout the state, it was awarded the state designation for the year as an "All West Virginia Town" It deserved it.

SOURCES

Colston, W. B., "Personal experiences of W. B. Colston"

THE BERKLEY JOURNAL, Berkeley Co. Historical Society
1977, Special issue

Gardiner, M. H. & A. M. , "CHRONICLES OF OLD BERKLEY' ,
1938 / currently out of print

HISTORY OF THE BATTLES & CAMPAIGNS OF THE SECOND REGIMENT OF VIRGINIA'S VOLUNTEERS INFANTRY – Manuscripts – Clarks Summit, PA – no date of publication

Howard, Carl, " The Mt. Clifton Hotel" Hedgesville Presbyterian Church , 2009

Moore, William D. Moore , HEDGESVILLE & THE CIVIL WAR, VOL
1 & 2, 1983 AND 1984

Moore, William D. Moore, "GLEANING FROM THE TOWN MINUTES"
1974

U.S. War Department – A COMPILATION OF THE OFFICAL RECORDS OF THE UNION & CONFEDERATE ARMIES, 1880.

Various Citizens - , "SENIOR CITIZENS REMINIENCE" Hedgesville
Senior Center Memories – 1974

Wyndham Family History – unpublished

ABOUT THE AUTHOR

William Dale Moore served as an elected public official for the Town of Hedgesville for twenty-four years. He was first elected as the Town Recorder but then went on to serve as Mayor.

He embarked on a task of bringing the town into the present day to make it a governmental entity that would enable it to survive in the modern world. The municipal laws were brought up to code, a system of fees and revenue was established, election rules were changed to WV laws, liaisons were established with the Berkeley County Commission, representation occurred with the Eastern Panhandle Regional Development Council, a professional study – The Comprehensive Plan – was done by Fox & Associates of Maryland, and the ground work was laid for future Planning & Zoning Ordinances to come later by others.

To instill as sense of historic identity & purpose, Mr. Moore proposed a celebration of the Town's 120th anniversary of incorporation in 1974. This became a five day celebration with several hundred people involved in a direct way to record and celebrate history and its background purpose. The stage was set.

The Town was awarded National Historic Registry status with several buildings being highlighted as historically significant. Deed covenants to keep the exterior of Naylor Hall the same were enacted by the Berkeley County Historical Society & Landmarks Commission.

Bill was awarded the highest Civil Award that can be given to anyone in the state when in 1987 he was made a **Distinguished West Virginian** by the Governor Arch A. Moore.

He wrote the first local historical study of the time period with "HEDGESVILLE & THE CIVIL WAR, VOL. 1, 2 in 1983 and 1984.

Continuing to write local history, he put together a brief sketch of the Mt. Lebanon Methodist Episcopal Church history. He wrote of a local industry, "THEY WERE NOT AFRAID OF THE WORK" - The story of the North Mountain Brick Yard, in 2003.

Although modest works, it ensures that the information will not be lost or forgotten

He was born in the hamlet of North Mountain Depot which is one mile north of Hedgesville. When he married Mary Kate Eckerd, he moved to the Town of Hedgesville where he spent the next twenty-nine years. Twenty-four of those years were as an elected official for the little municipality.

He graduated from Hedgesville High School and went on to receive a Bachelor of Arts Degree from Shepherd College (now Shepherd University). He taught English at Martinsburg South Junior High School for three years.

He went on to do graduate studies at Shippensburg University in Pennsylvania where he received his Masters Degree in Guidance & Counseling. He worked for thirty years for the Washington County, MD Board of Education.

Bill and Mary Kate had a daughter, Laura Andrea Moore. Together they restored and refurbished The Summit House a circa 1839 structure in the Town of Hedgesville.

He began another career as a Presbyterian Lay Pastor for the Tabler Presbyterian Church in Berkeley County, WV. He has been a Pastor there since 2000. The Eastern Panhandle Mission Council of the fifteen Presbyterian Churches awarded Mr. Moore an honorary Doctor of Divinity degree in 2011 for his leadership and pastoral service.

CPSIA information can be obtained
at www.ICGtesting.com
Printed in the USA
BVHW040218261120
594270BV00019B/634

9 781514 399446